Letting Go
to
Create a Magical
Life

Booklocker.com, Inc.
2009

Direct all correspondence to author:

PAT SENDEJAS

Post Office Box 4514 Westlake Village, CA. 91359-1514

E-mail: Pat@PatSendejas.com

Web site: www.fengshui4balance.com

Letting Go
to
Create a Magical
Life

Pat Sendejas

If the fear of letting go or loss keeps you from honoring your own or another's feelings, then you have separated yourself from the divine flow of energy, joy, and unconditional love.

Pat Sendejas

Acknowledgements

I am truly grateful for the loving support of my husband, Sal, who kept encouraging me to write this book. His strong steady confidence in my work became my anchor. To my talented editor, Victoria Giraud, I give thanks for her endless availability. Thanks Victoria for giving me those nurturing nudges to write more, uplifting words of encouragement at just the right moment, and to the laughter we shared helping to make this book a joy to write. Thank you to my mother who always believed in me and told me I could do anything I desired. In loving memory of my father who by his example taught me the value of positive thinking, perseverance, and to trust what you give away always comes back to you. Thank you to my sons, Christopher and James, family, friends, and clients who allowed me to share their personal stories to help bring clarity to this book.

Table of Contents

Preface

In August of 1995, I woke up with a jolt! I had been going through life as if I were asleep. So many things were not working in my life: especially my relationships and finances. Where I had hoped I would be at that point in life seemed like a distant and unachievable dream. I was saying yes to everyone, and never really checking in with how I was feeling.

Facing one challenge after another motivated me to take a closer look at myself, my behaviors, thoughts, beliefs, and relationships. It was the turning point of my life. What had worked for me years before: being driven, controlling outcomes, and setting goals, no longer worked. It was as though someone had changed the rules in the middle of the game.

These challenges were truly an awakening for me! I had been praying for an answer and as soon as I surrendered and let go, it was as if I had opened a floodgate. Information and answers began to come to me so quickly that I often felt overwhelmed. As a result, I began to slow down. I became more aware of the experiences I was having. I heard, felt and saw the world differently than I had heard, felt or seen it before.

Creating from a thought was not new to me. In my lifelong career of environmental design and architecture, I had to first have thoughts about a space before a design could be created and presented to the client. In addition, over the last few years I had begun to specialize in the "nature science" of Feng Shui that deals with energies that are invisible to the naked eye, yet have a tremendous impact on our lives. Although I was used to using the non-physical energy of thoughts to create and design, I did not totally realize how that same energy was contributing to everything I did and had in my life: from the relationships I drew to me, and the careers I chose, to the financial stability I enjoyed. And so it is with everyone.

As I became more of an observer instead of a "doer," I saw how surprising connections with people and events happened with amazing synchronicity. It seemed almost magical. Rather than trying to force and control events, I could step back and observe the results I desired. All I had to do was to think a thought with emotion and desire, let it go and observe how it would be brought back to me almost effortlessly in ways I could never have imagined, let alone planned on my own. I came to believe that if someone truly wants to improve his or her life, the act of "letting go" is paramount.

Introduction

In ***Letting Go to Create a Magical Life***, I plan to help you *let go* of any outdated beliefs about the physical world being all there is. What others have called "unbelievable," which you will understand after reading this book, I call everyday common occurrences for those who are willing to let go and allow something new and exciting to come into their lives.

Are you interested in *letting go*, in clearing the blocks, the resistance, in your life in order to move forward with ease to manifest your dreams?

Letting Go to Create a Magical Life tells you how. It will guide you to *let go* of old ideas and beliefs that no longer support you in the key areas of your life. When you do learn to *let go*, you will begin to experience amazing synchronicities, inspiration, and encouragement.

I will help you identify the thoughts, habits, beliefs, relationships, and fears that no longer serve you and may be holding you back. I have outlined opportunities and techniques to assist you in *letting go* in order to live a life that can best be described as magical.

Stories from my personal and professional life will enlighten you as you read this book. Learn how to move forward with your dreams by learning to joyfully *let go* using simple and fun techniques. Once I realized how important it was to become aware of my own feelings and to make self-supporting choices, the more fun I began to have.

As I look back over events that occurred in my life, which resulted in my own self-discovery, I understand the connection between what we are thinking or asking for, and what manifests in our lives. I realize there are no accidents; everything happens to move us forward, and what appears as a negative or a challenge actually serves as a catalyst. What we resist persists. What I was pushing to avoid was exactly what I attracted.

The wisdom I had been hearing for years and not taking seriously suddenly became obvious; what you presently believe becomes your reality. With the experiences I share in this book, I hope to raise the level of your beliefs. I now understand that what we think about and focus on with emotion expands and is drawn to us. I am still constantly amazed and exhilarated at the accuracy of this principle as it plays out in my life and the lives of friends, family, and clients.

I look forward to sharing my own exciting experiences with the magic of this energy. I hope these personal stories will help you become more aware and enable you to go from your mind into your heart, where your feelings reside, to improve relationships and create your own dreams and desires.

We carry the energy of creation within each of us. Great achievers have realized this. Walt Disney's message has always been about "the magic of believing." Martin Luther King said, "I have a dream." All creation begins from within each and every one of us, and this invisible energy of creative potential resides there. Those who realize this fact live a magical life.

Stuck energy within us causes blocks in our everyday life, and future chapters will elaborate on this resistance. Letting go of expectations placed upon others, of things no longer used or appreciated, including old habits, thoughts, and behaviors, creates a void, making room for new energy, new thoughts, and new experiences!

I will explain how this invisible energy within each of us becomes a vibration in our outside world and is seen all around us, connecting us to each other and supporting us daily. If you can get to a place of truly knowing who you are and what you desire, and then surrender to creating things "your" way, your life will become effortless. How do we get to a place of truly knowing who we are? By telling ourselves the truth about our feelings and then accepting those feelings instead of judging them, and avoiding any comparison of ourselves to others.

In **Letting Go to Create a Magical Life**, I will explain how this inner non-physical energy appeared in my physical world. I began to realize that every time I had a thought based on some strong inner emotion, such as fear, joy, exhilaration, or satisfaction, I would see those emotions manifesting as experiences in my physical world, and unfortunately, these experiences were not always what I thought I desired.

I began to learn that my reality and my experiences were also based on unconscious thoughts and emotions, of which I had been previously unaware. I began to question everything that occurred. "How did I create this?" I would patiently ask, and sooner or later I got my answer.

Chapter by chapter, my book will elaborate on how I interacted with this non-physical energy and how the answers to my questions began to come in for me as I asked and let go. For spiritual awakening to happen, the ability to ask for help is critical, along with having the desire to receive an answer. For example: a question could be, "What do I need to be doing that would create an endless stream of wealth, use my gifts and talents, and enable me to enjoy the work and improve the lives of the people with whom I come in contact?" Once you have asked and let go, it is important to trust and allow time for events and people to line up with your desire, bringing you effortlessly what you have asked for.

The person who is able to surrender to the fact that they do not have all the answers, and asks within their own mind, allows an energy field to form, which becomes a vibration that attracts a solution. My meaning of *vibration* is to create within you a heightened movement of energy produced by an emotion such as excitement or joy.

Excitement or joy tends to bring a positive solution; fear and anger tend to bring about what is unwanted. I have seen how the answer comes almost as soon as the question has been asked. When you're asking, the answer is already partly contained within the question. Just as important as asking the question is the ability to be open to the answer, letting go of how the answer comes and what that answer will be.

Having Positive Expectations

How you ask the question is important to the outcome. Asking the question: "Will I fail at this business venture?" is based on fear. Asking the question, "How will I celebrate my success when I have clarity of my new career direction?" is based on joyful expectations. Are you approaching your life positively with positive expectations?

I had a rewarding experience of asking and allowing the universe to bring in an answer when I was helping my mother find a new home after my father passed. I wanted her to sell her home of thirty-five years and relocate to a community near me. She had always expressed an interest in my community, and I knew of a townhouse area where I felt she would enjoy living.

While her house was for sale, I kept my eye on potential homes by walking my dog daily around the preferred area. Even though my mother hadn't yet found a new home the week her house sold, I wasn't discouraged. My husband and I drove to the desired location, and when we found nothing appealing for sale, we stopped near a row of townhouses while I pondered.

A few minutes later, I noticed three women coming out of a townhouse: one of them was carrying a vacuum cleaner. Taking the opportunity to ask questions, I got out of the car to speak with them. "Do you live here?" I asked. When they said no, I wasn't discouraged and asked, "Do you know anyone here who is moving?" One woman replied, "Yes, we are! We have been renting the home. Since the owner has chosen to sell it, we just finished cleaning it after moving out." She agreed to take my card to give to the owner when I told her my mother was looking for a home in the area.

The next day, the listing realtor called me. My house hunting in previous months had produced several homes that my mother put offers on, and yet there was no successful result until my mother let go of her attachments to her previous home. When my mother was comfortable with her decision to move forward, to let go of her home of thirty-five years, and to allow another to come in, the time was ripe and her home was sold. It was as if the Universe had orchestrated the entire event, like doing a dance with this delightful invisible energy.

All I had to do was ask for what I wanted—that my mother live close to me—observe how things would unfold, and receive. Ask, observe, allow, and receive; ask, observe, allow, and receive. Any action that is taken is inspired action based on what feels good to do, and does not require actions to control the outcome. The whole experience of creating is put into motion by the asking. The key to success was my detachment: I had let go of what was coming and how it would be revealed. Having the belief that I could receive was critical. The clearer I got about what I wanted, the easier things came to me. I got better and better at asking questions of my inner self and then allowing the answers to appear.

***

I have shared my personal stories over and over again at seminars and with clients and discovered these stories inspire, give hope, and often spark something personal within those listening. I am grateful to the people who have shared their personal truths with me. Their truths have added to my understanding and I, in turn, am sharing them with you.

Each chapter of this book covers a subject you may never have considered before, or you may have felt these concepts weren't important to your life. I encourage you to revisit these familiar ideas as if they are brand new. If you're open to new ideas and willing to participate in the simple exercises at the end of each chapter, you'll definitely benefit from this book.

Be sure to begin reading this book by *letting go* of any preconceived ideas as to whether or not you will have success with this different way of thinking.

Part I

*

The Magic

of

Energy

*

Chapter One
Invisible Energy

The world is what we think it is. If we can change our thoughts, we can change the world. H.M. Tomlinson

As I began my newfound quest to learn and work with this magical energy, "letting go" and allowing, I attracted Feng Shui, the traditional "nature science" from China, based on the invisible energy around us, into my life. It allowed the world to open up to me and I began working with new clients and a new way of communicating my ideas to the world.

Visible vs Invisible Energy

All substance and form is energy. It is yin and yang, the motion of the sun, moon and stars, everything that emerges and dissolves. It is the clouds, the mist, the fog and moisture. The heart of all living beings, all growth and development is energy, wrote Chinese philosopher and naturalist Lu Yen.

Physical energy is easy to see and contemplate as Lu Yen points out. Energy changes form but it doesn't disappear. It takes energy to make change; everything in our daily lives is in constant change. The sun rotates around the earth, day turns into night, plants change and grow, our children grow up almost overnight, it seems. What a remarkable phenomenon! We see the outward physical changes, whereas the invisible processes our bodies go through, like prayers or thoughts, is that movement of energy beyond our physical eyes.

In 1995, when my husband and I took our German Shepard to the vet, I witnessed a powerful demonstration of energy transformation. Pepsi was an adult dog we had brought home from the animal shelter. Seven years later, she was physically challenged by hip problems, which had been painful for some time and we knew we were probably going to have her put down. I was so upset and sad about losing her, I left to wait in the car and let my husband stay with her. I cried as I thought about our wonderful dog. Not long after, I noticed a large ball of shimmering white light of energy that suddenly appeared in the car right in front of my face. Seconds later, the ball of energy took off like a speeding jet. I was so surprised I wasn't sure what had just happened. Then it came to me: It was proof that my dog had gone back into pure positive energy. Her physical body had stopped functioning, but her spirit, the non-physical energy, had soared.

We have the potential to feel this energy, and we are impacted by it. The missing link in being able to manifest your desires is to understand the invisible field connecting each of us and everything around us in our universe. ***Letting Go to Create a Magical Life*** relates to how the non-physical came into my awareness and is now an integral part of my life.

Some may call this invisible energy God, as I had, using prayer to ask for support. Others refer to it as Source: where all energy originates. Some refer to it as Spirit, and others call it Universal Energy. For the purposes of this book, I will refer to this energy as invisible. I respect all the religions of the world and see that they all have a common thread, but my book is not a debate over which religion is correct or that you must have a religion to be connected to this energy to have a great life. In fact, you cannot be separate from this energy, because it is the energy that created us and our entire universe.

Emotion is a Factor

Emotion is the principal force that moves this invisible energy. Incorporated in the word emotion is "motion."

One day I decided to test my theory about how our emotions help us create. I started by getting in a positive mood and then picked up a spiral notebook and pen and went outside to my patio, close to nature, where I always feel good. After relaxing in a comfortable chair, I cleared my mind and asked myself, "What would I like to do to have fun?"

In my mind, I began to picture attending a wedding. I really got into this exercise by describing on paper how much fun I would have. It would be a wonderful experience where everyone in attendance would be joyful and loving toward each other. I described the wedding as quite extravagant and taking place in a beautiful environment, with dancing and music, and delicious food. I savored the experience and relaxed into the daydream, then I closed my notebook and let go.

Within a few days I received an invitation to a bridal shower at a beautiful home where the food was delicious, the outdoor setting was beautiful and the bride and everyone attending were happy. The invitation was not for a wedding, but it was a hint of what was to come, like seagulls let you know you're nearing land if you're on a boat in the ocean. I knew I would be receiving an invitation to a wedding. I was surprised when I received more than one invitation.

A week or so later I received a wedding invitation for October 1st, six weeks after my original journaling. Then my mother received a wedding invitation from her former neighbor, who she had not seen in years. She wanted me to accompany her. Both weddings were scheduled on the same day, though at different times, so I could attend both. And I did.

I took my mother to her friend's wedding, held at noon on a chartered yacht in Marina del Rey, California. We cruised around the harbor, enjoyed music and food and watched the loving couple exchange their wedding vows at the ship's bow.

At 5 P.M. that evening I was attending an outdoor wedding ceremony at a beautiful country club near my home. The ceremony was followed by a social gathering, where hors d'oeuvres were served before the guests were invited into a ballroom to be seated at elegantly decorated tables. A delicious meal was served, followed by music and dancing. I thoroughly enjoyed the entire experience of both celebrations: the joyful feelings and camaraderie, the music, the food, just as I had pictured it.

The most surprising event happened that same week in October. I had made plans to meet Donna, my friend from Maui, in Las Vegas on Thursday, October 6, and looked forward to enjoying a relaxing time together at the hotel spa. Donna also had plans to attend a co-worker's wedding that same week. When the bride discovered I would be meeting Donna in Vegas, she invited me to her wedding as well. My third happy wedding was set in an outdoor garden, followed by a sit-down dinner inside, with dancing and music following. The joy and feeling of connectedness between everyone was exactly what I had asked for. I had never met the bride or groom before, yet I could not have been more graciously welcomed to their special event.

My experiment worked! I had written down exactly what I felt would be fun and enjoyable and focused on the emotion of the event I wanted to experience. What I received was even better than I had imagined.

Creativity through emotion was demonstrated again when I listened to my friend Eric describe how he had met his wife. He told me he had learned how important getting into the feeling was in creating his desire. When he was in college, he had made a list of all the qualities he wanted in a girlfriend. He soon met a girl who had all the qualities he listed, but he discovered quickly she was using drugs. "Time for a new list," he said to himself. His new list required a girl who did not use drugs; even though this time his girlfriend met all of his requirements, she was also a constant liar.

Eric decided he needed to get into the right feeling to create a new love, the perfect partner for him. Remembering how wonderful he felt in his old jeans, he thought the perfect girl would feel as comfortable to him as he felt when wearing those jeans. "I feel very relaxed when I'm wearing them, like I'm on vacation, and I'm joyfully spontaneous in them," he told me.

Once he was clear on his feelings, and let go of his need for a list, it wasn't long before he met that great girl. He had been married to her for thirteen years when he shared his story with me. "Oh, and by the way," he added, "her name is Jeannie!" That story has stuck with me, and when I had the opportunity to meet Jeannie, I found she was indeed comfortable to be around.

Exercise 1:

Think of something you really enjoyed; like a trip to Disneyland with your family, a trip to a wonderful destination overseas, your wedding or the wedding of a close friend, a first trip to Las Vegas when you were dazzled by all the lights. Maybe your joy came from a time you enjoyed nature while camping with your family or friends, or the time you won a door prize, or won something you really desired.

Now that you have the event in mind, think about what you did and how you felt. It is particularly important to observe and remember your feelings. Write what you were feeling on a piece of paper. Was it the feeling of love, passion, excitement, or exhilaration? All of these feelings carry motion with them. While daydreaming about the experience, you may notice the good feelings moving through your body, the very motion that creates more of those good things to come into your life.

It is important when you create to be able to connect with these positive emotions. If you can remember how those positive emotions felt, then you can recreate them when you want to attract something new into your life, whether it is a new relationship, an increase in income, or a terrific vacation.

Exercise 2:

Think about something that was embarrassing to you, or sad, or upsetting. Can you feel the emotion within your body? You may even feel pain in certain areas of your body. Your heart may start to race, or the muscles in your arms or legs may start to hurt. It is important for you to become aware of the movement of this emotional energy going to various parts of your body: this non-physical energy. You can feel it, but you cannot physically see it.

Whenever you notice your attention has moved to something unpleasant in your past, you can journal about it until you have exhausted the feelings, or you can choose to change your focus and turn to something that is pleasant, preferably something you are looking forward to, something you are excited about creating, or doing. Either way, you are doing what it takes to be able to "let go" of the experience, journaling until you are tired of recalling the event, or thinking about something pleasant. It could be a trip, a home remodeling project, or something as simple as attending a party or going to a movie. Be sure to recall a pleasant thought that evokes good feelings before moving on to the rest of this book.

Exercise 3:

Using the positive feelings and emotions you have just recalled, take a spiral notebook and pen to a quiet peaceful place and sit down and relax. Whether it's a favorite spot in your home, the beach, a place in nature, your garden, or the local park, make sure it's a place you will be able to totally relax without being interrupted. Begin by asking yourself, "If I were to do something that is really fun and enjoyable, what would it be?" Allow your mind to wander. If you have any thoughts that distract you, allow them to float away from your mind.

Now is your opportunity to write your own script, your opportunity to write it the way you would like to live it. For this first experience, choose something you believe could happen rather easily. As you start to get a picture of something that would be fun to do or have, allow yourself to experience that through your emotions. Feel the excitement, joy, and passion, allowing any feelings about your desire to come forward. Begin to journal the experience in detail. When you have completely exhausted yourself with every detail and really felt the emotions of the experience, put down your pen and close the notebook. Now let it go. Do not attempt to think about how this experience may come into your life. The key here is to let it go and allow it to be brought back to you.

Chapter Two
Awareness – Know Yourself

I don't know the key to success, but the key to failure is trying to please everybody. Bill Cosby, Actor and Comedian

My life came to a challenging crossroads in 1995; I was saying yes to everyone, even when I really wanted to say no. My relationships were superficial because I was trying to avoid hurting others, and I did not realize that I did not know how to enjoy the moment. Even my finances were in shambles because I couldn't say no to the ones I loved. Looking back now, I see that I was giving my power away to please others. I had been doing this most of my life and thought that by behaving this way I was contributing to a better, friendlier, more loving world.

My misconception was that by giving to others before myself, I would have great relationships. Not only were my relationships failing, I was also sending a message to my sons, by my example, that they **should** take care of everyone else before they took care of themselves. I have since learned to become aware when I, or other people, use the word **should** in conversation. There is little room for creativity when we use the word **should**. It locks you into doing something without factoring in your own feelings about it first.

The word **should** conveys an element of control from the person who speaks it, implying that there is only one way to feel or act about the issue being discussed. I recommend you become more aware of when and how the word **should** is used in your life. Your awareness will help you be more in the flow of life and you will automatically begin to avoid any sentence using the word **should**.

When the word **should** is used, it factors out your feelings about the matter at hand, often putting the feelings of others before your own. The New World Dictionary defines the word **should** as an auxiliary used to express: an obligation, duty, propriety, necessity, etc. Putting the feelings of others before your own does not work, whether you are a parent or want to create quality relationships in your life. I know now that we must start with respect for ourselves or we will have none to give to others! Only then will you be able to truly help others, give back to society, and have respect for those you love.

I have found that when I have stress in my life, I may slip back to using the word **should**, even when I know better. Noticing this helps me bring my life back in balance by making choices that help reduce the stress. When you tell yourself you **should** do something, it is a form of manipulation to take action. Watch when you use the word and realize that it tends to be something you have been taught to do, rather than something you are inspired to do.

Try is another important word. Begin to notice when you or someone you are working with uses the word **try**. When someone says, "I will **try** to get that done for you," they are implying they really do not want to do it. Wouldn't you rather hear someone say, "I plan to do that for you by tomorrow?" See how much clearer the second sentence is to your understanding? There is no doubt in your mind that their intention is clear. The word *try* implies a lack of belief that the task can or will be accomplished.

The New World Dictionary defines the word *try* as: to make an effort; attempt or endeavor to accomplish something. There is nothing in the definition that implies an act will be successful or carried out to completion. If you want to accomplish anything, it is important to be aware what you or others are saying. In order for success to occur, your words and actions need to match. If you listen closely to the words spoken by yourself and others, you will be able to realize your true intentions and theirs.

During that challenging time of my life, I began to understand how to work with this invisible energy in order to feel connected to people and experiences, and what some might call "being in the flow." I learned the importance of letting go of my need to plan, rescue and attempt to find the answers for someone else. I learned to let go of negative thoughts, limiting beliefs, and old habits. When I was truly able to let go of being in charge, I gained valuable wisdom, and I would notice that I would receive support and answers in ways I would never have imagined. I learned that letting go is a natural process. As I began to go with the flow, my life became richer and more enjoyable than ever.

As I began to pay more attention to feelings I was having and events that were occurring around me, I heard, felt and saw the world differently than I had before. Surprising connections with people and events appeared with amazing synchronicity. It seemed magical because it was as if I could actually step back and observe the world rather than trying to force and control events to get things to happen the way I wanted them. All I had to do was put my attention on a thought with heartfelt emotion and desire, let it go, and then observe the manifestation of that thought in ways I never could have imagined, let alone planned on my own.

The law of attraction works whether you believe it or not. With my strong desire to make a difference in the world, I took it to an extreme: helping others to the point where I adopted an attitude that I needed to rescue people. As I became more aware, I realized I would often attract victims, allowing me to rescue them. Unaware of my need to rescue, I thought I was just helping others. I came to realize that when you step in and help others, who are capable of helping themselves, you reinforce their victim mindset, reinforcing their lack of confidence in themselves. Life is like an Easter egg hunt. The discovery is the fun part. When someone else tells us where the eggs are hidden, it takes the joy out of the adventure of life.

I learned that what was in my life was a mirror of my thinking. If I wanted to rescue people, then I would need to attract people who had a desire to be rescued. Just as a teacher who enjoys teaching attracts students who want to learn. Or a detective, who enjoys solving crime, first needs a criminal to commit a crime. Life is like a play where we can experience who we choose to be. If we do not like who we have become, we can choose to let go and change. It is our human perspective that determines for each of us individually what works for us and what does not. We play our part until it no longer serves us, and then we can choose again.

I noticed that oftentimes rescuers and victims come together so that each can play out their part. I had a therapist who told me once, "If you want to rescue, volunteer at the pound, because people are built with a guidance within that helps them know what is best for them." That was great advice and when I let go of the need to rescue, I was able to share, teach, and serve with no attachment to the result. I attracted positive and successful people into my life who were willing to learn and take responsibility for their own choices.

My relationships became healthier because I began to act from a place of confidence in the ability of others. The need to rescue in order to feel needed in order to be loved was replaced with the desire to just be. My fear for another's safety, success, happiness, or any type of worry, was now replaced with a new attitude toward others that all is perfect according to what each of us is choosing. This shift brought a loving allowance that everything is always perfect and brings wisdom we could never have allowed if we had interfered with another's choice. Life is a gift and if we make decisions for others, we take away their self-esteem and initiative.

When one person stops rescuing in a relationship, or one stops acting like a victim, the relationship must change, causing the other to change, or to find another partner who enjoys continuing the experience of victim and rescuer. Oftentimes, we are afraid to give up the role of victim or rescuer due to the fear of letting go and losing the relationship along with the behavior that is so familiar. When a relationship is truly based on love, people are encouraged to grow and change, and are allowed to be themselves.

Being in Alignment to Receive

If you are asking for improvements in someone else's life and you are in the vibration of receiving, you will get numerous answers, synchronicities, and all sorts of great information coming for the person for whom you are focusing. Answers will come to you, and yet nothing may change in the life of the person for whom you have asked, unless the other person's desire is a match to what is being asked for. The asking needs to come from the person who desires to benefit from the asking.

We have heard numerous stories that when people reached out in desperation and asked God for help, all kinds of support came for them. The big lesson in these examples is the ability to ask and let go. When people call out for help and ask, or pick up the phone and reach out for answers to their challenges, the answer comes in very fast, especially if they are able to let go of how the answer will appear.

The asking creates a desire, which moves energy and summons all kinds of information, people, and events. You then receive answers. When the person you are asking for lacks the desire to experience or receive anything different and is comfortable with their present experiences, nothing will happen. There is no way you can create success for someone else, unless the other person just doesn't care what happens to them, or they take an active part in joining you in the asking.

Asking for another, without their permission, only works when the receiver is in alignment with the question or desire being summoned. The person must take action to receive once the answer comes. If the person is not asking for help, what has been attracted disappears. If they were not asking to have a solution or answer, they may not be able to change their vibration to a receiving mode and will block the good from coming to them. Having a strong willingness and desire to receive what is being offered is very important.

The perfect example of asking for another and having it work out positively was when I asked for music to come back into my son James' life in a positive way. I had been experimenting with the law of attraction to see if our thoughts and asking really do work. I found a large cylindrical can for my "God can" and I had fun decorating it. I put a slit in the top so I could deposit folded notes of paper inside, and placed the can on top of my desk. Each morning I would write about something I desired, fold the piece of paper, let go of the desire and drop the note in the can. It became part of my morning habit in order to stay focused and get clear about how I wanted to create my day. The key factor here is that my son loves music.

A couple of days later, my sister-in-law, Janice, phoned and asked to speak with James. I told her she had just missed him and she could page him and speak with him directly. She said she would, and then said to me, "I have tickets I would like to give him to attend the Rush Concert." I told her I was sure he would like that. A day later I was outside gardening and realized why she offered James the ticket. I had put on my note: "I want to have music come into James' life in a positive way." I was clearly unattached about how it would occur. I did not care how it came in, and I did not even remember asking until a day or two after the phone call with Janice.

My older son Chris was also a fan of Rush at the time, and told me: "I would have loved to have received the tickets." I got my "God can" and showed Chris the note asking for music to come in for James, which explained to Chris how James got the tickets. Even though Chris loved Rush, he was not asking for tickets at the time. I specifically asked for James, and James was in alignment because of his love for music. Chris understood how easily we can manifest our desires just by the asking and was able to let go of any resentment about James getting the tickets instead of him.

If you are spending a lot of time focusing on someone else and how they can move forward: a spouse, child, or friend, you are taking the focus off yourself. It could be you are hesitating to ask for help for yourself. Whatever you feel the other person needs, at the time you're asking, is probably what you need and are now ready to receive. Ask yourself why it is so important that the person you are focusing on needs help from an outside source. Once the answer comes, it is important to turn the answer around and apply it to yourself. If you are related to the person you want to help, you can do them the most good by changing yourself. Changing yourself changes the cells in your vibration and also changes other generations in the past and those to come. Your changes have a domino effect and all those who come in contact with you will change in some way as well.

Often, we think if people we love are different, it would make us happy, not realizing that our own true happiness comes from our inner self. By focusing on others, we avoid what we need to do to make ourselves happy. If we feel we would be happier if our spouse had a better job, or our kids went to college, we are basing our happiness on external conditions. Once we let go of the attachment to the desire, we become more loving, more allowing, and non-judgmental. Then we can allow the invisible to bring in something that could be even greater then we could imagine. Once we realize we just don't have all the answers and it's alright, we start to live our life in the moment, letting go of the control, and having more appreciation and joy. Relationships improve, and our life takes on a natural flow.

Angels all Around Us

Once again my "God can" attracted a happy ending. I was working with my design client, Carol, to prepare her thirty-year-old home for the Community Wellness Home Christmas tour. It was a tour of six homes in the area that were opened to the public on a Saturday and Sunday to raise money for the

Cancer Society, an annual tradition in our community. It was the first year my client had offered her beautiful home for the tour. She had numerous storage units for all her Christmas decorations and collectibles she had acquired over the years. She decorated every room and had three large decorated trees throughout her home: one with musical ornaments, another with ornaments that had moving parts, and another with personal ornaments she had collected over the years.

Carol started in early November to prepare for the weekend event. I told her I would not be able to attend Saturday; I would come on Sunday. On Saturday morning, the first day of the event, I was getting clear about what I wanted to add to my God Can. I had been told we have lots of angels all around us and if we do not ask for what we want, their energy is wasted. They desire to help us, but do not choose to interfere in our life unless asked for help. So I wrote to my angels and asked that they watch over my client and help her to have a successful event and that everything would go smoothly for her.

Later that day I called Carol to find out how things went. She told me there had been a crowd; people lined up out the front door. When she maneuvered her way through the line to the front door, a man in line tapped her on the shoulder and pointed to the smoke coming from a nearby lamp. She quickly realized a fire was just beginning, called the fire department and cleared the people from the house. All her decorations had overloaded the electrical circuit in the house. Amazing, I thought, if she had exited a minute earlier, she would have been gone from the house. Had an angel been there tapping her on her shoulder? She certainly thought so.

The fire department discovered the fire had started inside the wall, and could have been much worst if not caught immediately. She told me she was in tears because she had to close the house for the rest of the day and disappoint the people who had been waiting in line. Fortunately, an electrician attending the tour offered to stay and help repair the damage. She was able to open the next day for the tour and all turned out well. Time and again, I have seen how asking and letting go helps us to create magical moments.

Letting Go of the Need to Please

Here is a great example of something that was arranged for another that resulted in the opposite of what had been desired, demonstrating how asking for another can backfire.

A woman had a daughter who taught school and lived in Prescott, Arizona. The daughter came to visit her mother every summer on her teacher's summer vacation period. Her mother lived in Phoenix. Four years after the daughter began her teaching career, she came home to visit as usual. This time her mother, who worked at a local school, saw a great summer job opportunity for her daughter: teaching for a couple of weeks. Although the daughter loved teaching, she had been looking forward to vacation and spending time with her mother. Although she agreed to take the job, she couldn't wait for it to be over.

When the mother lined up a teaching job the following summer, even though it was only for four days, the daughter once again agreed, reluctantly. The night before the last day of teaching, the daughter expressed her frustration to her aunt since she was unable to tell her mother she felt she had earned a break from teaching. On her way to teach that last day, she almost ran her car through a red light, and when she suddenly stopped, her car rolled into the oncoming traffic lane and was hit from the side by another car. No one was hurt, but she was stunned and upset.

Her mother was notified and came to pick her up, and she did not finish her last day of school. When questioned later, she admitted she had told her aunt she did not want to teach that last day.

This story reinforces that our emotions play a strong role in creating our reality. Her reluctance to teach the last day was enough emotion and creative energy to attract a way to keep her from reaching the school. Her subconscious kept her away without harming anyone. What looked like an accident was the law of attraction in action, the end result of her asking.

The need to please others needs to be let go. The need to please is very counterproductive to having the life you desire.

The poem below by an anonymous author really sums up how important it is to be your own best friend.

The Guy in the Glass

> When you get what you want in your struggle for self,
> And the world makes you king for a day,
> Then go to the mirror and look at yourself,
> And see what that guy has to say.
> For it isn't your mother, your father, or wife
> Whose judgment on you, you must pass.
> The fellow whose verdict counts most in your life,
> Is the guy staring back from the glass.
> He's the fellow to please, never mind all the rest,
> For he's with you clear to the end.
> And you've passed your most dangerous and difficult test,
> If the guy in the glass is your friend.
> You may be like Jack Horner and chisel a plum,
> And think you're a wonderful guy.
> But the guy in the glass says you are a bum,
> If you can't look him straight in the eye.
> You may fool the whole world down the pathway of
> years
> And get pats on the back as you pass,
> But the final reward will be heartache and tears
> If you've cheated the guy in the glass.

> *Author Anonymous*

Who Are You?

Over the years working with my design clients, I became concerned with what I perceived to be my clients' dependency on the external to provide their happiness. After spending the last few years going within to figure out who I am, I did not want to mislead my clients. I realized that I, and many others, have been searching outside the inner self to find happiness, making the process of self-discovery difficult.

I came to realize that the external choices I made were also part of who I am. When I started to identify with my own likes and dislikes and not only accepted those choices, but embraced them, I became more relaxed and comfortable and realized how to be my own best friend. When I stopped searching outside myself for answers from someone else, and checked in with my feelings, it became clearer to me who I am; life choices became easier to make, and with those choices came peace for me. I began to understand and accept that, to my clients, changing their environment was often like buying new clothes, a way to express who they had now become. With that new environment came joy, confidence, and a feeling of comfort for them.

Seeking to balance the internal desires with the external helps to create a life of clarity. Being aware of our feelings and desires is how we develop our personal intuition. By choosing to start from a place of love, peace, and joy from within, this magical energy flows effortlessly. Within daydreams are great creations. Fear and criticism of ourselves tends to stop the flow of energy, preventing events from occurring as well as blocking the flow of our own abundance of time, love, money and all the things we long for in life. As we long for things, we often overlook the gifts we already have. I, for one, missed many of the joyful moments of life by overanalyzing instead of allowing spontaneous creativity to flow. In those moments of spontaneity are great abundance and joy!

All creation begins from within. Letting go of expectations placed upon others, of things no longer used or appreciated, including old habits, limiting thoughts and behaviors, creates a void, making room for new energy and new experiences!

As Helen Keller said, *No pessimist ever discovered a star or sailed on an uncharted sea or found a path to the human spirit.* What you think about and what you focus on expands and is drawn to you. I am constantly amazed at the accuracy of this principle for the friends and clients for whom I consult.

To discover yourself at a deeper level, it is important to acknowledge that your relationships are a mirror for you to determine who you are. Your environment: the furnishings, accessories, and colors are also a mirror of how you feel, and what you are thinking about. Your environment is a reflection of the thoughts you have daily.

People are brought together in relationships and environments because they have similar thoughts. If you seem to be attracting the same challenging experiences and unsatisfying relationships over and over again, you may want to ask yourself, "What do I need to learn from this experience? What role am I playing in this relationship?" If you do not like who you have become, then it may be time to let go of your behavior, or let go of the relationship. With the obstacles we encounter comes the opportunity to find our truth: to discover who we are!

Sometimes deep inside, people feel they do not deserve to be successful or happy, so they choose a partner who is not compatible with their life goals. Then they can blame the partner for their lack of accomplishment. It is healing to realize that you attracted the partner, parent, brother, sister, friend to you for the relationships and the experience of realizing who you are. Letting go of blame, anger, resentment, jealousy, and any emotion that does not bring you joy is your secret to success. If you are having a hard time understanding why you are in a relationship that does not bring you joy, ask why you attracted it. Then allow the Universe to bring you your answer. I know you will learn a lot about yourself when you ask the question and are willing to hear the answer.

It is said that the person who pushes your buttons the most, perhaps even the most challenging person in your life, is your greatest teacher.

To create balance in your life, an awareness of your own personality and preferences is crucial.

Exercise 1:

To help you get clear about your own preferences, take out a piece of paper and begin by making a list of events in your life that made you giggle. List things throughout your life, from a very young age until now, that brought you pleasure, joy, or laughter. As you make your list, notice if you were doing something with someone, or were you alone? Was it a passive activity like sitting by a lake and fishing, or was it an activity like swimming or skiing? Begin at the earliest age you can remember and think of joyful moments. Write them down.

Take as long as you need to get as many activities listed as possible. Once the list is complete, go back and see if you have similar activities reoccurring over and over all your life. If not, you may be the type who has to have lots of variety. Or maybe you have to be doing something creative: building or designing. What about people? When you were having the most fun, were you with family, friends, or co-workers? Or were you all by yourself?

Remember not to judge the experience, just allow yourself to get to know your preferences: likes and dislikes. This exercise will help you make quicker decisions for yourself in the future. Our experiences give us information about what we enjoy and what we dislike. To experience something and fail is far better than to have never experienced it at all.

Exercise 2:

This exercise helps to change unwanted habits. If you have someone with whom you spend a lot of time, it would be helpful to ask them to help you with this exercise. This will help you realize how your words may be holding you back from moving forward to create a magical life. Words are a reflection of your thoughts and habits. Ask someone to keep track of every time you use the word ***should* or *try***. If you are caught using either of these words, then you will need to give up something in order to become more aware and change this habit. You might choose to put $1 in a jar for a charitable donation, or give up something important to you each time you are caught slipping.

I heard on TV that a famous actress used this technique by having her father catch her in a behavior she wanted to change. She had two small children and wanted to stop cursing. To stop the habit, her father suggested she let go of something important to her, like the frequent purchase of new shoes. Because she loved new shoes, she quickly changed her bad habit.

It is important for you to select something you care enough about losing that motivates you to change your habit. Practice this exercise over a twenty-one-day period, because studies have shown it often takes a minimum of twenty-one days to change a habit. If you are consistent, you will begin to change your thoughts and your words.

Exercise 3:

This is a simple exercise to help you form the habit of focusing on creating what you want each day. In this chapter I refer to using a "God can" because it helps to remind you that "God can" handle your requests. You may choose to name it "Angel can" or "Spirit can", just find the best way for you to reinforce the action of letting go and turning your requests over to the invisible. You can name your can anything that resonates with support. Find a shoebox, glass jar, or a large can.

Your container needs to have a lid and be large enough to hold at least fifty folded pieces of paper. Cut a slit about two or three inches long in your lid. When you begin your morning, sit for ten minutes and jot down on a piece of paper whatever comes into your mind that you desire for that day, week, or month. If you have children, you can get them in the habit of doing this before going to bed. Let them decorate their container and make it a fun family project. Each person needs to have a separate container and it is best not to share the experience you asked for until it has occurred.

If you are new to this method of manifesting from your thoughts using directed intention, I suggest you start with simple requests, because you will get faster demonstrations and increase your belief in the process. Some suggestions: write that you would like to experience laughter throughout your day, that you would like to receive a surprise phone call from someone you have longed to speak with, or perhaps receive an invitation to a party or for a lunch date. Just as I had asked for music to come into my son's life in a positive way, your request must not indicate how the demonstration will appear. Let go of all attachment to the result.

Once you have written one request on a piece of paper, fold the paper and put it in the container and forget about it. Do not think of the request again. You may be surprised at the requests you wrote, and how many actually become part of your daily activities. Make as many requests each day as you would like during the ten minutes you spend. After a week or two, you can pull out your notes and review what you had written.

Remember to visualize the activity and think about how you would feel if it occurred. Remember that joyful feelings and thoughts about your desires create faster results. Anything that has not been created can be placed back in the box or replaced with a clearer intention.

Chapter Three
In the Moment

Living consciously involves being genuine; it involves listening and responding to others honestly and openly; it involves being in the moment.

Sidney Poitier, Actor and Author of *The Measure of a Man*

I am realizing now how often we get what we ask for without realizing we've asked. Our thoughts and our subconscious mind are very powerful. Within our thoughts and feelings lies our intuition. By becoming more aware of our thoughts and feelings, we can choose to take inspired action that moves us in a supportive and magical direction.

During an ocean cruise with my husband, I became aware of the undeniable intuition within me, which motivated me to act. My husband and I charged $799 for a four-day ocean cruise on a department store credit card and went for a short trip. The first day on board I had a deep desire to play bingo and a deep intuitive feeling that we were going to win. "I know you are going to win, buy some cards to play," I told my husband. Because of our limited funds at that time, he hesitated at first, and then he bought one for each of us. I was so amazed when I won that I had a hard time speaking up. The winning pot of $600 was to be split among all the winners, but I was the only winner! My winnings helped pay for most of our trip.

The universe seemed to be saying, "You'll be OK; there is abundance all around you!" Could it be that when you trust your own feelings, you will be supported in what you ask for? I now believe so. I think this is the way things happen to all of us, all the time. Joy opens the energy and allows it to flow. Anger and fear shut down the energy and cause blocks, delays, and struggles. We do not fully see the big picture, we take things for granted, and we forget to be thankful. We are not aware of this incredible concept of creation being possible to each and every one of us all the time!

My answers began coming rapidly and almost out of nowhere. I began to start asking questions in my mind. I learned it's not the answer that's the most important; it's the question we ask. A perfect example of this happened to me one night as I was writing my first book, five years after my bingo experience.

I asked myself, "Why did I win $600 and not $700 or $799, which was the cost of the trip? What was the reason for the $600 amount?" That night I had many dreams, none relating to the $600. The next morning I was flipping through a dream book when I came across the interpretation for the symbol of $600. "$600 – 6 is your guidance, higher teachers, (teachers of light): pay attention." Once again I got my answer within hours. The $600 was a symbol of support, not just financial support but spiritual as well.

It was incredible that every time I asked a question, the Universe provided an answer to my question. At that moment I realized how important asking is to the life we are living. I realized that those who never ask, never really connect and communicate with the invisible energy of infinite possibilities that is all around us all the time. I also noticed that it took me five years to ask why I won $600 and not some other amount.

It had not been easy for me to allow someone else to help me, or to be able to surrender and trust. I have seen how letting go creates magic, joy, and abundance. What you give away comes back to you. When our actions are based totally on unconditional love, for ourselves and others, it is returned back to us tenfold. Every time I let go of being right, or doing it "my way," I find I experience greater personal growth.

In 1995, I first became aware of this magical energy, this creative force and great intelligence operating to protect and guide each of us on our path of experiences when my husband and I attended a four-day self–discovery seminar.

The day before we left for the seminar, for some reason I asked Sal to look closely at my wedding ring to make sure the diamond was secure. It was an odd request since I had never worried about the stone. I had taken the ring to be cleaned and reset about five years before, and I had worn it for twenty years before that without any concern.

Outside the seminar room of the hotel waiting to go in, I began talking to a woman from Colorado. Our husbands joined us and we walked over to an adjacent area where I sat down on a cement bench. As I listened to my husband and the other couple, I felt my wedding ring, and to my surprise it felt as though the diamond was missing.

When I looked down and saw that it was gone, I was not upset and remained seated. I remember feeling quite calm and remarked matter-of-factly to the couple, "The diamond is missing from my ring." Their reaction, however, was quite anxious and they made suggestions about where I might have lost it. "Could it be in your car, or in your hotel room?" they asked. Still surprisingly calm, I remained seated and looked around. I spotted something sparkling on the cement about ten feet away from me, and wondered if it could be my diamond. I walked over and picked it up, almost as if I knew it was there all along. I have been told "nothing is lost in the universe," and now believe that to be true.

When I rejoined my husband and the other couple, I showed them my retrieved diamond. The woman said to her husband, "Dear, you remember that tiny zip-lock bag that the earphones were in on the airplane yesterday. I asked you to take it with you, and you didn't know why, but you put it in your pocket anyway. Give that to her for her diamond." The little zip-lock bag in his shirt pocket was perfect for safekeeping my diamond and ring.

The seminar began as Dwayne, the speaker, drew a picture of a diamond on a large easel. "Are you familiar with the diamond?" he asked as Sal and I glanced knowingly at each other. Then he said, "It is the most precious stone you have. The diamond is like your magical child. It is the most precious thing you carry with you. Most of you have lost your magical child, but you will find it this weekend at this seminar!" I felt like I had just been tapped on the shoulder by someone who really wanted to get my attention.

An Enlightening Dream

At home after the seminar, I had a life-changing dream.

My mother and I were on a beach being guided toward a large blanket where other mothers, their children, and siblings were gathered. Once there, I was asked to come to a classroom where I would receive the certificate for completing the weekend seminar I had just finished. One of the program directors directed me to the classroom. As I hurried across the beach, I lost a shoe. "That's OK, my shoe isn't important," I said to myself.

When I found the upstairs classroom, I took a seat and noticed there was a podium where the graduates would be announced. I looked down and saw my other shoe was missing. "That's OK," I told myself again. "I mustn't worry about how I look and what people think, that's not who I am." When I heard them call my name, I walked to the front and turned to see the audience. My son and my mother were missing, and when I asked about my son, I was told he had a choice about whether to come or not, and he had chosen not to. I felt I had to find him, but I was worried if I went alone, I'd get lost. Too impatient and worried to wait for help, I ran out of the room and down the stairs onto the sandy beach.

Suddenly, I came upon my unshaven son wearing a red-plaid shirt. "I'm so glad to find you," I told him. He held up his thumb and forefinger and declared, "Mom, you were this close to me before on the beach, and you didn't even see me!"

When I woke up, I realized I had been missing the most precious moments in life. I had been so busy filling up every moment of my life with work or busy activities that I was choosing to avoid and deny my true feelings. I was with my family in physical form but my mind was always in the future, planning and creating, never able to stop long enough to enjoy and appreciate what we had as a family, or experiencing and appreciating each other for our uniqueness. I recognized then that spending time with people I love is the most precious thing I have.

The moment is all we ever have. I had missed many precious moments and loving words because I was too busy to stop and listen—really listen—with my ears, my eyes, and my heart. Now I look at every moment as a gift. It wasn't until I let go of having to be right, and having to be the one with all the answers, organizing, planning, and controlling each situation, that I was truly able to see the magic in each moment.

Exercise 1:

Give yourself about a half hour for this exercise. Sit down in a quiet spot where you will not be interrupted. Once you are relaxed, think about someone in your life who has made a positive impact on you. This person can be dead or living. Even if you feel you have shared your feelings with this person, write down all the things that come to mind about them that have made you grateful for their influence on your life.

If more than one person comes to mind, you may want to write about a different person each day in order to give this exercise the importance it deserves. Once you have written your list, contact the person and share how you feel with them. You may be surprised at the positive impact this exercise has on their life. If the person is deceased, read your list out loud to yourself or someone close to you. You may be surprised at the positive impact this has on your own life.

Chapter Four
Ask

One of the lessons I've learned is that the quality of the answers that we get in life are truly determined by the quality of the questions we ask.

Paul Martinelli, Speaker and
President of Life Success Coaching

I could not deny that the Universe was bringing me answers as quickly as I could ask the questions. The events happening around me were too obvious to ignore! I could see clear evidence there was a direct connection between what I was thinking and asking for, and the wonderful abundance that began showing up in my life. I am confident there is an intelligent energy force that surrounds us and is always communicating with us, if only we would be still and allow the miracles I call magic to appear.

I began to meditate as often as I could. Never previously able to sit still for very long, I found it to be a wonderful, addictive experience of peace. The silence of going within gave me answers and daily guidance. I also noticed that if I got lost in the task at the moment, like gardening, I would begin receiving intuitive thoughts. I also discovered the writings of Neale Donald Walsch and spent time listening to a series of audiotapes of his best-selling books: *Conversations with God.*

Validation of asking and receiving was appearing all around me! I was no longer the only one having these magical experiences. Friends and clients began to share with me wonderful stories of how their thoughts and desires had manifested.

My friend, Donna, in Texas, told me how she had wanted to take a trip to Florida with her husband and son and to stay in a house on the beach for one week. She had asked, in her mind, for $400 to make that vacation happen, sharing those desires only with her husband.

Donna and her husband decided to have a two-day garage sale one weekend to raise the money. Their actions showed their true intent. By taking action, they put their desire in motion, creating energy to make it happen. Not knowing how much money their belongings might bring, they trusted their desires would be met, letting go of any attachment to the outcome.

Besides household items, Donna had gathered together many items of clothing to sell. Some of her son's sweaters looked so new, it was as if he had only worn them fifteen minutes, she joked. On Sunday, when the flow of people tapered off, they started packing up what was left. Just as they had finished, a family with five children drove up. They didn't appear very prosperous and were specifically looking for clothes.

Surprised that they had sold very few clothes all weekend, Donna decided to simply give the family all the clothes for free and then helped them load the trunk of their car with the items. Donna told me it was as if the clothes were being saved for this very family.

After they drove off, she counted the money she had taken in over the past two days. She had never checked the money or attempted to count it; she trusted the outcome and let go of all control over the result. When the total came to $401, she told me she had a good laugh. What made the weekend sale special was giving the clothes to a family who loved and appreciated them. "If I knew it would be that easy to get the amount of money I asked for, I would have asked for more!" she told me.

I imagine the family who received the clothes had been asking for those very items prior to finding the clothes, just like Donna was asking for her vacation money. Neither the family nor Donna knew how it was going to manifest itself.

A few years later, in the summer of 2001, Donna called me early one morning and said, "I want to relocate to Maui, and I would like you to check on air fares and come with me while I interview for a new job." I told her I would see what I could do, but I was not very experienced in booking travel reservations.

That evening, while relaxing in the spa with my husband, I shared Donna's plans and her request that I investigate travel arrangements. I said to him, "I would love to go with Donna to Maui. I wish I could get air fares for $250 each, then I would go."

I never gave that desire another thought. The next day Donna called and said she had lined up an interview and she was going immediately. I wished her luck in her interview. She got the job and over the next two months she prepared to move to Hawaii.

My husband and I were also moving, and when we closed escrow on our new home, I spent a couple of months remodeling the entire house. We had purchased the home in August and in September we were getting ready for drywall to be done. I called a firefighter who owned a drywall business to bid the job, and when he arrived, he asked if we were going to Hawaii for the special price offered to L.A. City Firefighters by a local travel company. "No," I told him, "I don't think I can leave in the middle of my construction."

This firefighter told me it was a wonderful opportunity to go and that during the drywall work I would not need to be present. He inspired me to discuss this further with my husband. The offer was a special thank you to local firefighters. Many from L.A. City had gone to ground zero in New York after 9/11 to help with the cleanup from the disaster at the twin towers. After much discussion with my husband, we decided to go to Hawaii. We had two choices of destination: Maui or Oahu. This was the perfect chance to visit my friend Donna, who was now living in Maui.

We decided to request Maui, but discovered Maui had been completely booked. When my son found out, he told us, "I will check for you with my neighbor who is vice-president of the travel company offering the special." We got a call from our son saying that everything was taken care of. It was a fabulous trip. When we arrived at the airport in Maui, we were provided a car for the entire week of our stay; our hotel had been upgraded to the Ritz Carlton on the beach, with a price tag on the room door of $1500 a night. Unbelievable as it seems, the cost of flight, room, and rental car came to–$250 per person, a total of only $500.

I remembered back to that evening in the spa just six weeks before when I said to my husband, "I would love to go to Maui, if the cost was only $250." What we say, feel with emotion, and then let go of, comes into our experience if we are willing to "let go," allow, and receive. There was no way I could have orchestrated all this by controlling the outcome.

The Surprise Delivery

The computer arrived in forty-five minutes, even though my client was quoted three weeks! That event was an example of how fast we can bring in what we are asking for when we are clear and willing to receive. If we ask with a strong belief and let go of the results, it will occur.

When I met with my business client, I began by asking her to tell me about her and her husband's desires. Her husband worked at a bank full-time and was attending school to be a computer animator. She was looking for the ideal location in their home to place the recently purchased computer in order to support creativity and learning for her husband.

I asked to see the computer, and she told me they did not have it yet. They had purchased it and it was being assembled, to be delivered in about three weeks.

"When do you want to have it?" I asked. With great emotion and no hesitation, she declared, "Now!" I replied with complete confidence, "And so it is!"

I know if someone does not hesitate, and can answer my question clearly, what they wish will be brought to them quickly. I must admit I did not expect it to be at her door while I was still there. To my surprise and hers, it arrived within forty-five minutes.

It is important that a person know exactly what they want. I have found the hardest task for most people is to be clear about what they want! Anyone can create if only they believe they can! Believing for most people is the hardest task. Why? Probably because we have been taught from our childhood that thought is more pretend than reality. We have been taught that life has to be difficult. We look at our past, and based on that limited experience, we often create our present. We repeatedly make untrue assumptions of the present and continue to create based upon those incorrect thoughts! Life is what you believe it to be!

Abundance shows up in our everyday life and circulates back to us when we give unconditionally. I took my parents to a motivational lecture, and on the way home my father wanted a milkshake. As I drove to a nearby ice cream place, I was focusing on creating a balance between my giving and receiving. I planned to treat them, but when we got out of the car, my mother said immediately, "I would like to treat!" My parents always wanted to treat; over the years they continually refused to take anything from others. I reminded myself I could be a lot like that as well, and I decided to graciously receive.

As my mother and I went inside to order, the girl behind the counter was looking at two different cash registers. It was almost as if she were trying to decide which one to use. "It's free, right?" I said jokingly to her.

"Do you want it for free?" she asked. Quite surprised at her question, I had no doubts and I replied, "Yes, that would be great!" She went back to make up our order: ice cream for the three of us.

My mother was astounded when the girl offered to prepare three orders of ice cream at no charge! Meanwhile, the next customer came in, the other employee took the order and money was exchanged.

The girl preparing our order grinned widely as she handed us the three milkshakes at no charge. We thanked her repeatedly and left. My mother and I were delighted at this unexpected experience. My father was puzzled: How could this have happened?

At that moment I realized that when you are able to receive, not just give, you bring joy to others as well as yourself. That ice cream server had been quite pleased to give us the free order, as pleased as we were to receive it. Since the experience was unexpected, I was not attached to the results. I had no prior expectations; I was just enjoying the moment. Our benefactor was so pleased to be able to surprise us with her gift that her joy was contagious. I knew what I wanted and was able to ask for it. Once we become clear about what we want, ask, let go and allow, then magical moments filled with fun and abundance happen!

The experience of receiving free ice cream was proof the Universe provides in ways we could never believe possible. When we base our beliefs on past experiences, what others tell us, or on what we have been taught to believe about how the world operates, we continue to wonder why things are not changing in our lives. In order to allow the Universe to support us, we must change, let go of the thoughts that limit us. In order to do this, it is important to recognize the things that come into your life demonstrating your abundance. As you recognize your abundance, magical happenings begin to occur. As I began to notice my surroundings and experiences, I would reinforce the experiences, as good things began to come to me, by stating my gratefulness with enthusiasm.

I began increasing my abundance by recognizing the small stuff. For example, when going to dinner I would order a salad and always notice that my salad was the largest on our table. I would joyfully say things like: "Oh, look how abundant I am," or "I am abundant," or just simply, "Thank You, God." I noticed when I ordered takeout food, I ended up with more than I had ordered, like nine pieces of chicken when I only ordered eight. By noticing the little things and being thankful, I began to bring in a larger and larger share of abundance. Friends and family found it difficult to believe what was occurring.

Exercise 1:

Are you a giver or receiver? Do you always have to be the one to give? Often, giving gives us a feeling of control over others, or gives us a feeling of power over our own circumstances.

Perhaps you feel sorry for others and feel you need to take care of them. This exercise will help you create balance in giving and receiving. The best way you can gain more abundance in your life is to be able to receive as much as you are able to give. If you tend to be the one always receiving and being taken care of, then it may be your turn to give. Let go of the idea that others need to take care of you. By giving more, it shows the Universe you trust there will always be enough in your life.

Decide if you are fearful of giving or receiving. Decide if you tend to be out of balance in one or the other. Then spend the week giving spontaneously if you have determined you are a receiver, or spend the week receiving if you tend to be a giver.

Give in accordance with your income and your level of trust. Do not do anything that will place you in financial hardship or anxiety. Just be aware of what you are giving and receiving, and how you feel about it. This exercise is to increase your awareness of how you experience life.

Do you only give when you feel you have more than enough? Do you give compliments easily? When you have a desire to give, do you act spontaneously or analyze first before giving? Observe any self-talk going on in your head.

Ways that you might give: Ask to pay for the car in line behind you as you drive through a fast food location, or offer to pay for the coffee or the ice cream order when in a snack shop. How about a smile or a positive acknowledgement to someone who may need a lift? At first you may find changing a habit feels very uncomfortable. How about offering your letter carrier a soda or bottle of water? If you have a favorite charity you always give to, why not increase your donation, or choose an additional charity.

Be prepared to receive. When offered a compliment, immediately say thank you and don't debate the compliment. When a friend wants to buy you lunch or treat you be gracious and accept. Watch to see the benefits that come to you as you seek balance in the area of giving and receiving.

Chapter Five
Believe

The thing always happens that you really believe in, and the belief in a thing makes it happen.　　Frank Lloyd Wright

Our beliefs about how much things cost and if we have enough money to afford something is what keeps our abundance at bay. Over and over again, as I began to believe in the possibilities, I have received services and products for free or at reduced rates. A few years ago, while I was redoing my website, I got a referral for an Italian-based web designer from a person helping me create some promotional products. I contacted the designer through the internet. After making a substantial payment and working for several weeks to convey my ideas and establish a direction, I still did not know how to use the web software he was using and also realized I would not be able to edit my own site once it was completed.

I felt conflicted about the experience; it wasn't going in the direction I wanted. Although I knew the web designer was good, I also knew I needed to honor my own feelings. I decided to forget about what I'd already invested. I told him I could not continue and wanted to settle my bill.

I let go of working with him without knowing who would design my site. I just let go and allowed the Universe to guide me. To my surprise, a business associate working to maintain my client e-mailings offered to finish my site in a program that would allow me to be able to do my own editing. The wonderful part was that he helped me create and finish my new website with no additional charge.

If you are emotionally charged about something, it will bring things to you more quickly. If you are arguing, the emotion of the energy can draw in something you may not want.

Why do We Block our Receiving?

In December 2008, I was complete with my book. The entire book was with my editor for a final paper edit when I picked up the January 2009 edition of "O," the Oprah magazine, in the beauty salon. As I flipped through it, I found an article by Holly Brubach entitled "Are You Ready for Change?" No coincidence there. I had been looking for ways to help people let go. The article was about a pair of Harvard educators, Robert Kegan, PhD, and Lisa Lahey, EdD, experts in adult learning at the Harvard Graduate School of Education. They had spent twenty years wondering why people don't change. The article contained a brief description of an exercise these experts use to help people identify their blocks. Their exercise inspired me to create a similar exercise for my book and workshops. You will find the exercise at the back of this chapter.

My own personal experiences confirm their information. In this book, I have written about how our strong desire for success isn't always followed by achieving what we desire. Despite our great sincerity, oftentimes we will find ourselves going in frustrating circles instead of fulfilling our goals. Some have referred to this condition as fear of success, but it goes much deeper than that. We are protecting ourselves by doing everything we can to avoid the fear, disappointment and pain we feel are associated with the achievement of our desires. I discovered certain experiences I continued to remember that were associated with unwanted events from my past, and until I became more aware of the triggers that were caused by my pursuit, I would do anything to avoid the experience. I was working hard to achieve my goals, and yet missing the mark.

When we become aware of the triggers that cause our self-sabotage, we can consciously replace the trigger with a positive action or thought. This process is often done in hypnosis. For example, a person who wants to quit smoking might be told that the desire for a cigarette would be replaced with the desire to eat an orange. To achieve your goals, the first step is to identify what you want. What would bring you the most joy? What are you doing, or what have you done to achieve your desire? Ask yourself if there is an action you repeat which seems to be in conflict with your desire. It can be something very subtle, like not giving yourself enough time in the morning to get to work or school and being late, even though you say you want to be on time for work or school. This is a clear indication that something in your subconscious is working in opposition to what you desire. The same is indicated if you make an appointment and then forget about it. It looks like an accident, although in your subconscious mind it was done intentionally. Become aware of these incidents and you will become more aware of your true dreams and desires.

When I looked closely at my actions, I could see I was sabotaging what I desired. I wanted to do seminars attended by lots of people, providing me with an opportunity to do what I enjoy, sharing information and teaching. I had often been invited to speak to groups of 200-500 people, so speaking to large groups of people was not an issue. It was apparent to me that I was not avoiding the speaking itself. When I began planning my own seminars, I realized I scheduled them quickly, not giving my potential participants the time to plan their schedule in order to come.

Once I traveled to Hawaii, searched for a classroom to rent, scheduled a Feng Shui seminar, signed the contract for the room, and sent out information for the seminar, all in one week's time. What was I thinking? With such short notice, I ended up with a very small audience, perhaps no more than four! Advanced notice with advertising and marketing several weeks or months in advance would probably have resulted in a larger audience.

Through a past life regression I later learned I had made a promise at my death not to teach people how to work with energy. Just before I died I remember begging not to be killed as I said, "I won't teach people about energy again." In this life, unaware of the promise I had made at the time of my death, I was keeping that promise not to teach energy again. So my Feng Shui classes about energy were taught to a smaller audience. I was subconsciously avoiding advertising my classes about energy and not giving my audience advanced notice, totally unaware of the inner agreement I had made.

Once I became aware of the agreement and how I was sabotaging and limiting my success, I began to plan ahead, making sure I gave people more than enough time to plan to attend my events. This result can happen to people when they say they want to have more relationships or fun activities in their life and then sabotage themselves by sending invitations at the last minute, or never bothering to make the call to set the date. Awareness of what we say and do, I discovered, will reveal the limiting beliefs ready to be cleared.

Our beliefs contribute to our actions. If we feel, for instance, that relationships take too much time, and we have a hidden belief that we just don't have enough time, or if we believe that relationships involve too much responsibility and we are seeking a more carefree lifestyle, then, even though we say we want them, we take subtle action to avoid them based on our fear of commitment, disappointment, or a belief in a lack of time. Once an underlying limiting belief is identified, it is important to replace the old belief with a more positive one in order to let go of the old. Hidden beliefs, however, may take days, weeks, years or a lifetime to uncover if we are not willing or ready to look at ourselves and take responsibility for our experiences.

Our beliefs greatly influence what we create. I realized that when someone else would do the scheduling, advertising, and promoting of my seminars, they were filled and ran smoothly. Having someone else do that was a big factor in their success, even though I would do what needed to be done, I did not enjoy being the one who always had to plan and schedule and find a location and advertise and promote the event. All I wanted to do was show up and do what I do best, share information.

Often, when I mentioned this to people, they would laugh and say, "Wouldn't we all like that." I took that to mean that I might as well forget that idea, and yet, that inner desire, kept haunting me. Every time the desire surfaced, I would tell myself, that can't happen, you need to get busy, and I would push away those feelings of what I really desired: support in planning. I was stuffing my real desires and creating a situation where I could say: see I really don't do this well. I need someone to do this for me.

We all want to be right, and to prove our inner beliefs are right, we create our reality to justify our beliefs. What is so great is that when we have the limiting experience, we immediately know what our limiting beliefs are by what shows up in our life. When it isn't what we are asking for, it becomes a red flag indicating a belief that we may choose to replace. By taking responsibility for what shows up in our lives, and being honest with ourselves, we can let go more easily.

Once the belief was identified, I realized how it was not appropriate to the life I am living. I began to let go of my resistance, and just proceeded to do what I needed to do. That is the act of allowing. The process of growing spiritually requires accepting what is, without resistance, all the while confidently trusting in what we desire to show up along our journey. That is when the support arrives. Once we stop resisting what we do not want, the focus is put on what we do want. Then we see what we have wanted showing up in the most magical ways.

I did what I needed to do, though I continued having a strong desire to find support. One day I got a call from a woman who worked at the location where my seminar would be held. She said, "I received your flyer, and called to tell you that we do all the registering and promoting through our center, so you won't need to do any collecting. All signups go through us, and I will be taking care of all of that for you." Wow, just what I had been asking for and it came when I accepted what I needed to do, and let go of my resistance of how it might come in.

Having someone doing what they do best in scheduling and promoting was a dream come true. Now here is the key. Find your dream and focus on it. You won't know how it will come in, but the point I want to make is that now you have a key ingredient in manifesting your future. You know what to ask the Universe for. I received clarity about the fact that I was avoiding teaching about the invisible magic of energy to protect myself, and yet I was not allowing my good to come in because I had another hidden belief that what I wanted was just impossible to have. Nothing is impossible for God to create.

Hidden Beliefs Revealed

When you have discovered the belief that is interfering with your desire, all you have to do is ask for what it is you really want and then allow yourself to receive it. If you are unable to receive it quickly, you may have another hidden belief that needs to be cleared. You may not realize that everything happens in its own time, not necessarily exactly when you want it.

Looking back over my life, I realize I had deep desires attached to my values, especially my family. Nothing could keep me from achieving certain goals, but they were occurring in the proper order and time, unfolding as I deeply desired. The first thirty years of my marriage were very important to me and reflected my higher values of spending time with family. I would not compromise my family time, for anything, even growing my career. Family was my number one priority. Many parents are hard on themselves when their new business or career is growing at a slow pace. If asked, "If you had all the money and all the time you desired, how would you spend your time, building a career or spending time with your family?" many would choose family. Neither one is good or bad, just very revealing. Once they understand that their most important value is family, they can let go of growing the career at that time. Others may find they are experiencing depression from subduing a deep longing to pursue a successful career that will give them an outlet for their talents.

The secret to having that magical life is being honest with yourself about what you really want and how you feel without judgment. When you admit to yourself what you want without judgment, you will know what to ask the Universe for. Letting go is easy when you are clear about what will bring you the most joy. You must believe it is possible. Because of my values, my career was secondary. Knowing what our values are and honoring ourselves brings a feeling of calmness and confidence.

Many things influence our movement toward our goals, both positively and negatively. The priority of our values has the greatest influence on our experiences and our success. The beliefs you accept from others, often referred to as the collective consciousness, and your environment from birth are great influences. The traumas imbedded in our cells from our past may cause us to avoid what we feel could be harmful.

When we believe in ourselves, know our values and what we want, and we feel the deep inner knowing that what we want is achievable, we are in alignment and our life changes almost overnight.

Change may take time because it involves a five-step process; pre-contemplation, contemplation, preparation, action, and maintenance. Once you have identified the new behavior, it is good to reward yourself as you choose to take a different action. Do not expect successful results to come with the first attempt to change. Take small steps and let go of when and how the new behavior will bring the success you desire.

Exercise 1:

It is important to know and be honest with yourself in order to create a magical life. Prioritize the following values, with your first choice on top: doing the right thing, money, control, helping people, family, friends, education, learning new information. Do not judge the order you choose, and do not pick what you think would be socially acceptable.

Write down what you feel you would like to create for your life after you get clear in your mind what it is you truly want. What would bring you the most joy? Consider what you are doing, or have done to achieve your desire. Ask yourself what are you doing that is in conflict with your desire. Ask yourself how you sabotage your goals.

List the things you do that could be keeping your goal from occurring. For example, you may resist clearing your clutter at home or in the office. The clutter problem could be keeping you from experiencing something you fear, like: making an important decision, working on a project that feels overwhelming or beyond your ability, or the fear of throwing something of value away that you believe you might need later, lacking a trust within yourself to easily obtain the information again. All of these fears are based on underlying beliefs. Once you have identified the belief, you can decide what action you can take to change. Start with small steps to gain comfort in your new actions.

If you need help changing the habit, don't hesitate to ask the Universe to send you someone to help. Then watch for someone to appear. Allowing someone to help you is a sign that you are able to receive, and it gives you practice to allow the support. When you allow the support from others, the Universe continues to send you more blessings and support.

Leave yourself encouraging affirmations on your bathroom mirror, by your nightstand, or in your car to remind you of your newly desired action. Be good to yourself, knowing and allowing for a relapse. If you find yourself going back to the old habit, be sure to replace it with your newly desired behavior as soon as possible.

If an action you need to take is something you do not want to do, consider a person who would help. Be willing to pay for help from others, and trust that your time is valuable. Remember, if the task is something you do not enjoy, you may be avoiding it on an unconscious level, and that avoidance can cost the achievement of your goal. You now know what it is you will need to receive, so go to your "God can," as explained in Chapter Two, and add what you need. The Universe is waiting for you to ask. These requests could include having a wonderful job in a great environment doing only what you enjoy, having a very supportive assistant to accomplish what you don't prefer to do, or having a loving and supportive relationship with someone you trust and with whom you feel truly connected.

Exercise 2:

Creation follows thought. In this exercise you will be able to get clear and allow yourself to see that what you are asking for is already present in your life. Take a piece of paper and write what you want at the top:

(Use one sheet only for each desire)

Below, on the same side of the paper, list the reasons why you want it:

Leave the whole bottom of the paper to write all the feelings you think you would have if you had it. Be sure to focus on the feelings.

On the backside of the paper, write the reasons you believe you already have it:

It is said that even before you ask, your desire will be answered. Creation follows thought, which follows perception. If you can perceive that you already have what you are asking for, it will be easy to keep that desire coming. It increases your belief of possibility. Intuitive counselors see how you are living and believing today and are able to reasonably predict a similar situation occurring for you. An honest intuitive will tell you that you can change anything you are experiencing by changing your thoughts about it.

For this exercise, if you want to have a better relationship with someone, write down your desire. Example: I want to have a better relationship with my neighbor. Write why you want it. Example: It feels good to have someone you know and can count on living close-by. It is feels good to know people care. It would bring a feeling of safety knowing my neighbor. List all the feelings you would have if you had a better relationship with your neighbor. Turn over the paper and list all the reasons you believe you already have what you desire. Example: My neighbor waves when I drive by. My neighbor is respectful of my sleeping hours. I have asked to borrow some eggs from my neighbor and they were glad to loan them. My neighbor helped me find my lost pet. This exercise will help you increase your belief about having what you want.

Start this exercise with desires that can be validated, which also helps increase your gratitude and brings in more of what you   desire.

Exercise 3:

This exercise is important to do without analyzing. Just complete each sentence below with one word.

1. People who are rich are
    _____.

2. Teenagers who drive new cars are
    _____.

2. People who have a college degree are
    _____.

3. People who shop a lot are
    _____.

4. People who leave their children with babysitters are
    _____.

5. People who take vacations every year are
    _____.

6. Women who are thin are
    _____.

7. Men who watch sports all weekend are
    _____.

8. People who go to the gym and exercise regularly are

_____.

9. People who go snow skiing are

_____.

10. People who play tennis a lot are

_____.

11. People who go camping with their family are

_____.

12. People who wear expensive jewelry are

_____.

13. People who sleep in late are

_____.

14. People who get up early are

_____.

15. People who work in an 8-5 job five days a week are

_____.

16. People who work all their life in the same job will

_____.

17. People who own their own business are

_____.

18. People who own their own home are

_____.

19. People who live in apartments are

_____.

20. People who wear glasses are

_____.

21. People who talk with an accent are

_____.

22. Men who have beards are

_____.

23. People that are tall are

_____.

24. People who are short are

_____.

You can make up your own sentences. You will find your judgment keeps you from having what you want. If you believe that people who have wealth are more likely to be workaholics, you may not want to have wealth. If you feel that teenagers who drive new cars are spoiled, you may not want to be seen in a new car.

This exercise is to show you how your mind judges and will resist having the very thing you say you want in order to avoid an underlying fear or to maintain a certain belief.

Chapter Six
Let Go

Learn to let go as easily as you grasp or you will have your hands full and your mind empty. Every hello is the beginning of a goodbye, but every goodbye can be the beginning of another hello.

A Vietnamese proverb from Leo Buscaglia's book,
The Way of the Bull. (Discovered by my editor)

In 1996, after twenty-two years of running my own interior design firm, I decided to slow down to spend more time with my family, and I began part-time work as a sales rep for a shutter company. As much as I liked that job, I ultimately desired a career where I could really make a difference in the lives of others.

Circumstances I hadn't planned on, like my brother's serious illness, gave me the impetus to let go of the sales rep job so I could spend time with him. I trusted that my job situation would work out. I also knew all we truthfully have in life is the moment. I would soon learn that letting go was the prerequisite for attracting something new.

Shortly before leaving for Phoenix to be with my brother, a friend gave me a book by Og Mandino called *The Choice* and also a book about Feng Shui. This was the first time I had heard of Feng Shui, and my friend was surprised since I had been in the field of design for more than twenty years. I was introduced to a new way of looking at the environment and interior design when I discovered and embraced Feng Shui, a "nature science." It became a tool that enabled me to understand and explain the magical energy I was beginning to experience.

I had been asking for work I would love, and I could soon tell I was going to choose Feng Shui as a new career. It was the perfect example of: *Ask and receive!* Not long after discovering: *Letting go brings abundance.* By letting go of my previous job, I created a void, which allowed room for a new career to appear.

When people doubt their desires are possible, it is because they have set up unrealistic expectations. When the expectations do not occur in the manner expected, doubt sets in. Having a wish, and letting go of any expectation for when or how that wish may manifest itself is the secret to creating magical moments and abundance.

I have experienced so many examples of getting what I ask for, I now have a strong knowing that what I want and think about with positive emotion will eventually occur, as long as I am willing to receive it and allow it to come in at the perfect time. Thought has been said to be like prayer: it is constantly manifesting our reality. I am much more aware of my thoughts now than ever before. I have learned that it is important to *trust* and *let go* of any attachment to how my desire will occur. I find the sooner I am able to let go of any attachment to the result; the quicker things come in for me. I monitor my thoughts to stay positive, replacing negative thoughts with positive ones.

The clearer you are about what you want in your life, the more it will show up in your experience. Becoming aware and having clear intentions is the key element in creating your life. Letting go of things no longer needed verifies, by your actions, you believe there is abundance and you *trust* God, or the creative life force of the universe, that all you desire will be provided, especially if you are able to let go. The law of circulation requires a balance between giving and receiving. When you give, you create a void, making room for more of what you desire to come to you. Giving and receiving is like exhaling and inhaling; it's the way energy flows, and it's important to keep in balance.

We are surrounded by invisible air currents and energy the Chinese call "Chi" that moves effortlessly around and through us, and is contained in all things, as within and around a building. Your thoughts, which can be positive and uplifting or negative and doubtful, are part of this invisible energy. If you have doubt, you will begin to block the flow of energy.

Michael Phelps was recently interviewed after he successfully broke the record for winning the most gold metals of any Olympic athlete. He was asked after accomplishing this remarkable feat, "When people said you couldn't do it, what was your response?" He replied, "That is when my imagination came into play along with hard work." His intention was clear and he never allowed doubt to influence his thinking. He was always seen before each of his swim events with an iPod and earplugs in his ears.

When asked what he had been listening to, he revealed it was music with the most positive lyrics to reinforce the thoughts of success in his subconscious mind. It also kept him from being distracted by other people's negative comments, the noise of the crowds, and any distraction that would have taken him away from his intent to accomplish his personal goal. Phelps found his own method to let go of negative influences that could have hindered his success, and helped to keep him in a positive environment. What do you do to create a positive environment for yourself?

Like Michael Phelps, you can choose to put yourself in a positive and uplifting environment. There are no victims, only people who choose to believe they are less than others. Everyone has the ability to choose positive thoughts or negative thoughts. The more positive thoughts you choose to think and tell yourself, the more you will enjoy success; the more negative thoughts you choose to think, the more your experience will be negative.

If you find yourself thinking the same thought over and over, this is evidence you are not letting go. Changing your thought is a choice you have in every moment. Changing your thoughts by training yourself to choose positive thinking, takes practice. Observing your thoughts and comments is necessary. When you have a negative thought be prepared to replace it with a thought that makes you feel better. Think of a positive thought ahead of time so that when you notice your mind wandering to any self defeating or negative belief, you can replace it immediately with a memory or thought that makes you laugh, or with a positive affirmation. Like going to the gym regularly or exercising daily, training your mind to be positive takes practice. What you say to others is very revealing about your beliefs, and attitudes. Notice if you are attracting friends in your life who complain about problems or are they positive thinkers.

Oftentimes, we look for experiences that reinforce our beliefs about ourselves. We perpetuate behaviors that do not support us because they have become comfortable. If you feel you aren't accepted by others, you'll attract people with the same belief. There's a feeling of security when you feel your belief is justified. Once a person is able to believe they are worthy with good intentions, people and experiences will begin to show up that reinforce their goodness.

The Value of Tranquility

The more tranquil a person becomes, the greater is their success, their influence, their power for good. Serenity – the last chapter from *As a Man Thinketh* - James Allen (Published by Barnes & Noble, Inc. 1992, pages 49-52)

Calmness of mind is one of the beautiful jewels of wisdom. It is the result of long and patient effort in self-control. Its presence is an indication of ripened experience, and of a more than ordinary knowledge of the laws and operations of thought.

A person becomes calm in the measure that he understands himself as a thought-evolved being, for such knowledge necessitates the understanding of others as the result of thought, and as he develops a right understanding, and sees more and more clearly the internal relations of things by the action of cause and effect, he ceases to fuss and fume and worry and grieve, and remains poised, steadfast, serene.

The calm person, having learned how to govern himself, knows how to adapt himself to others; and they, in turn, reverence his spiritual strength, and feel that they can learn of him and rely upon him. The more tranquil a man becomes, the greater is his success, his influence, his power for good. Even the ordinary trader will find his business prosperity increase as he develops a greater self-control and equanimity, for people will always prefer to deal with a man whose demeanor is strongly equable.

The strong, calm person is always loved and revered. He is like a shade-giving tree in a thirsty land, or a sheltering rock in a storm. Who does not love a tranquil heart, a sweet-tempered, balanced life? It does not matter whether it rains or shines, or what changes come to those possessing these blessings, for they are always sweet, serene, and calm. That exquisite poise of character which we call serenity is the last lesson of culture; it is the flowering of life, the fruitage of the soul. It is precious as wisdom, more to be desired than gold-yea, than even fine gold. How insignificant mere money seeking looks in comparison with a serene life- a life that dwells in the ocean of Truth, beneath the waves, beyond the reach of tempests, in the Eternal Calm!

How many people we know who sour their lives, who ruin all that is sweet and beautiful by explosive tempers, who destroy their poise of character, and make bad blood! It is a question whether the great majority of people do not ruin their lives and mar their happiness by lack of self-control. How few people we meet in life who have that exquisite poise which is characteristic of the finished character!

Yes, humanity surges with uncontrolled passion, is tumultuous with ungoverned grief, is blown about by anxiety and doubt. Only the wise man, only he whose thoughts are controlled and purified, makes the winds and the storms of the soul obey him.

Tempest-tossed souls, wherever ye may be, under whatsoever conditions ye may live, know this- in the ocean of life the isles of Blessedness are smiling, and the sunny shore of your ideal awaits your coming. Keep your hands firmly upon the helm of thought. In the bark of your soul reclines the commanding Master; He does but sleep; wake Him. Self-control is strength; Right thought is Mastery; Calmness is power. Say unto your heart, Peace, be still.

James Allen (1864-1912, Author)

The Blame Game

Our thoughts precede our experiences. If you do not like what you are experiencing, change your thoughts about yourself and your life. When letting go of a habit or pattern of thought, it takes time to allow for the change to occur. Then it must be reinforced with reoccurring positive results acknowledged by you. If you are angry or blame someone else for your misfortune, you may never move ahead to realize your success or happiness.

I personally experienced how letting go of blaming others resulted in a very positive outcome. This was demonstrated by what occurred shortly after moving into our new home. During our home remodel our realtor entered our name in a drawing at her real estate office for $1,000. The realtor who represented the sellers worked in the same office as our realtor and stopped in to see our remodel of the home they had recently sold us. During their visit, they asked if we wanted to fill out an entry form for their office drawing. I filled out the drawing slip again and did not give any thought to winning.

A couple of weeks later while we were removing walls, my husband suggested we move the mirror in the front bathroom, which was being torn apart, and put it in the master bath, which was not being remodeled. It seemed like a good idea to me, and we did so. Upon removing the old mirror in the master bath, we discovered mold behind the mirror and opened up the wall. Our contractor told us that when an electrical fixture had been installed, a nail had been driven into the wall and through a pipe, which caused a leak in the pipe and created the mold inside the wall. I noticed the leak at been repaired.

We took photos and had our contractor document the problem. We wrote a letter to the previous owner, and in their response, they denied knowing anything about the leak. They told us they would never have exposed their eight-year-old son to mold had they know about it. I was surprised since the wife had lived in the home since the age of nine and had purchased the home from her parents ten years before selling. Surely they must have known about the leak or at least the repair that had been done.

I gave a lot of thought about whether I should proceed. I considered how much time legal action might take and the stress it would bring to finishing our remodel and getting settled. How satisfying would it be to blame someone else, arguing who was right and who was wrong? It certainly would create chaos in my life, and I decided it wasn't worth it, to me, or to the sellers, to spend time in arbitration over this issue. I decided to let go of my complaint. I was hoping to have extra money to pay for this unexpected repair.

The next morning I received a call from my realtor: We had won the $1,000 in her office drawing! What surprised my realtor was that we won with the drawing slip entered by the seller's realtor. The other realtors in the office complained that the seller's realtor had been soliciting another realtor's client. I knew it was the way the Universe acted in our behalf, rewarding me for letting go and trusting that all would work out fine.

Environments Mirror the Occupant

Just as the relationships you choose reflect who you are, the environment is also a mirror for you and your thoughts. In a building, when we interfere with the natural flow of energy by blocking staircases with piles of stuff, placing debris behind doors, or stacking papers on the floor, we interfere with the flow of energy within that space. Occupants of such a building, an office building, for instance, may begin to experience sluggish energy around normal activities: delays in contracts being signed, phone calls not being returned, expected deliveries being late. These delays may result in wealth or health issues for its occupants.

One of the most empowering activities to improve health and wealth is the ability of the occupants within such a space to *let go*. Letting go comes in many forms. Letting go truly is an act of forgiveness for others and for us as well. By no longer thinking or talking about the activity, which is negative or perpetuates hurt feelings, we have "let go." Do whatever it takes for you to personally let go. Michael Phelps, who listened to reinforcing positive music lyrics before each swim event, will go down in history as the winner of the most gold medals won by an athlete in a single Olympics. What can you do to let go of the negative thoughts that replay in your mind keeping you stuck?

If we see that we cannot stop talking about or thinking about someone or some activity, then we truly have not let go and those feelings must be brought to the surface in order to be healed. We let go when we no longer go to blame, regret, resentment, and/or anger. We let go when we give up the excess of food and beverages that add weight, and reduce energy in our bodies. Be sure when you are letting go of excess body weight, you refer to your weight reduction as "letting go," "melting away the pounds," or "releasing the weight." Never say "I am losing weight," because what you lose can always be found again. You want to be sure you are letting go once and for all! When we hold on to these emotions in our bodies we feel fatigue, in turn throwing our bodies out of balance. Our buildings are just like our bodies. Holding on to *stuff* is symbolic of holding on to these emotions.

Donating is Letting Go

Donating is the perfect demonstration of letting go. I had a gift certificate, part of a balance owed from my speaking fee, to be used at the Hyatt Hotel in Palm Springs. I called to make reservations before it expired and was told that my $125 credit would probably be enough for two nights because it was during the off-season. I was scheduled to arrive on Sunday with my husband. On the Thursday before leaving, I sorted through all my books and took sixty-six hardcover books to donate to the library. I had quite an assortment, from interior design books and spiritual books to books on raising children and teens. Many of the books were from my past, when I had needed them, and I wanted to give them to someone who might now benefit from them.

When I got to the library, they gave me a cart for all the books. As I unloaded my car I was tempted to put some of the books back in my car. I resisted the temptation; if I had not read these in over a year, they would be best shared with others. I did not want to stop the flow of energy with things sitting in my house not being utilized to the fullest. That same week I also chose to give up my office in my home for my twenty-one-year-old son, who wanted to move back home to save money and build up his finances for his own place.

When we checked into the hotel on Sunday, the hotel bell captain took our key and said, "My, this is a great room!" It was a suite with a living room, dining room, two bedrooms, three TVs, and two bathrooms, one with a bidet, and both with spa tubs. It also had three balconies: one overlooking the spa and two overlooking the pool. We had a fully catered breakfast in our room, enjoyed the spa, and the total bill when checking out was $23.23.

When checking out, my husband asked what the normal rate of our room would be, and the desk manager told him, "The room charge is usually $600 per night." I donated over sixty books, gave up a room in my two-bedroom condo, and got a $600 room almost immediately. I let go with no expectations and the universe provided abundance, creating wonderful magical moments! The $600, the same amount that I had won on the cruise, had appeared once again! There are no accidents.

The action of letting go demonstrates our trust. As we let go of relationships, habits, or stuff in our life that no longer serve us, we tend to feel out of control or insecure, and yet it is this action of letting go that demonstrates our trust. By letting go you may find unexpected people, things, or elements of nature coming into your life to give you a feeling of stability and support. Trusting, by living in the moment, provides the universe an opportunity to bring exactly what we need into our lives at the perfect time to support us.

Howard's Story

Trust was a critical part of the act of letting go, according to my friend Howard, who shared with me the pain he would have avoided if he had only "let go." Howard attended a weekend self-growth seminar, where participants had an opportunity to experience various physical activities to learn more about themselves. With a harness, which was attached to his body and to a crane for safety, Howard took the challenge to climb a telephone pole. He had to climb the rungs on the side of the pole until he reached the top. At the top, the climber was to stand up on a nine-inch diameter flat surface and then leap to a trapeze, which would lower the person to the ground.

Knowing his harness would catch him if he fell, Howard climbed up the telephone pole like a repairman, hugging the pole and attempting to keep his balance while going from one rung to the next. When he got to the last rung, he needed to maneuver himself up to the flat surface at the top. The difficulty was to balance himself on the small surface with nothing but the cable to hold onto. He told me he reached above his head to grab the cable and balance himself while he maneuvered into position.

So far so good. He was at the top and needed to leap for the trapeze, but he didn't feel stable enough to let go of the cable and leap for the trapeze. Suddenly, he lost his balance. All he had to do, he told me, was let go when he couldn't keep his balance any longer, but he kept holding onto the cable. Meanwhile, as he was falling, the cable was scraping his hands much worse than a rope burn. Because he wouldn't let go, he suffered second to third-degree burns. It had seemed to him, he told me, that it was like life or death at that moment, and he just could not let go.

Watching other people doing the exercise was nothing like doing it himself, he said. To Howard, the experience was like climbing stairs with a handrail and at the top there was no handrail. His mind played games with him and he was unable to let go.

The experience happened years ago, but when he recalls it, his hands feel the sensation and he remembers the burning pain. "It was excruciating pain, and all I had to do was let go." Letting go is so easy to do unless the emotions and the mind get in the way, Howard said. He was holding on for dear life because he thought he was going to die. Letting go was the answer, the key to avoiding the pain, yet he could not do it.

Exercise 1:

Carry a note pad with you throughout the day and write down every time you agree to do something you really do not want to do. You will need to become your own best friend. You will need to acknowledge your own personal feelings and trust how you are feeling for this exercise to be successful for you.

At the end of the day before going to bed, find some quiet time and review your notes. Take time to ask yourself, "What would happen if I had said no?" Are you coming from fear of loss that you may lose another person's love? Are you coming from a place of feeling obligated? Are you doing something you don't want to do because you have been told you should? Do you think you need to please others? Do you feel responsible for another's happiness?

Ask yourself these questions and get clear what it is that drives your decisions. If it is to please someone else, then you are not living your life to the fullest degree possible and you are denying yourself the opportunity to enjoy being who you really are. You are cheating yourself of life. The responsibility for your own happiness is completely up to you.

Chapter Seven
We Are All Connected

After taking the fences down from around our individual plots, we discover that there is only one field.
 Ernest Holmes – Founder of Religious Science

The Surprise Gift Came in the Perfect Moment

My mother told me my brother Russ had become quite ill. My parents went to visit him in Phoenix at the end of August for a week and then they returned home. My father had a hard time watching his only son die and chose not to stay through the experience. My mother called me the Monday she returned and wanted me to fly back to Phoenix with her.

On Tuesday I went to my work to tell them I was leaving town, and I didn't know how soon I would return, due to my brother's health. Oddly, my last appointment was at the home of a woman who had been a former Mrs. America. Her daughter and her father had been stricken with leukemia at exactly the same time, and she had been conflicted about whom to visit: one was in a Los Angeles hospital and one was in New York. She didn't tell me her decision, but in the end her father passed on and her daughter recovered.

This woman was now traveling and speaking to groups about her experiences. She gave me the book *Embracing the Light* by Betty J. Eadie. I read it on the plane to Phoenix with my mother. The book, which describes after-death experiences, came into my life at the exact moment I needed the information. I passed it on for my mother to read, and I know she was as comforted as I was by the information. When experiences like this occur, it reinforces for me how we are all connected.

One of the lessons my children taught me so well was the importance of listening, especially to people you love. Listening shows how much you really care. On the evening my mother and I arrived at my brother's home in Phoenix, my brother was having difficulty breathing and was asking for oxygen. My sister-in-law thought he could wait until the morning when she could order it for him. I sensed some urgency about his request and asked that we get him what he was asking for, so we all drove him to the hospital. They checked him in, and we started a waiting vigil. It was Wednesday, September 11, 1996.

The next morning his daughter Robyn was with me in the waiting room when the most unusual thing happened. Rosemary Altea was being interviewed on TV, and she claimed she received communications from people who had passed. I suggested my niece watch the interview because I had recently read her book, *The Eagle and the Rose,* and I had found it very interesting. My niece listened while Rosemary talked of a man who had died of cancer, and related how his spirit had hovered over the hospital bed and watched all his family before he died. He wanted them to know he was now happy and even had all his hair back. My niece was very comforted.

Had my niece been silently asking for help? She had attracted an experience that certainly gave her comfort. Was it

God that came through in that exact moment to give my niece what she needed to hear? I don't think it was an accident; it was a miracle. I believe my niece, without realizing, was receiving an answer to her thoughts and prayers. The timing was perfect.

The dictionary defines a miracle as: "an event or action that apparently contradicts known scientific laws and is hence thought to be due to supernatural causes, especially to an act of God." Again, I saw how we are all connected. Some invisible influence beyond our comprehension brought my niece together with Rosemary's sharing at a time that could only be described as perfection. Whether you credit the experience to God or creative unknown forces in the universe, the synchronicity could not have been overlooked.

Before leaving for Phoenix I had good intentions to massage my brother's feet to relieve his discomfort. I spoke with an intuitive healer who told me I would do some healing with foot massage. Before leaving, I phoned an alternative healer to find out the proper method, and when she told me to be careful because I could make his condition worse; I became fearful and changed my mind.

I discovered when I arrived that my brother was so ill my foot massage might not make any difference. He could hardly speak. To my surprise when I was in his hospital room, he pointed to his feet. It was almost as if he could read my mind. I asked if he wanted his feet massaged, and he nodded yes. After several minutes of massage, I went to the waiting room. His wife and daughter came to tell me the swelling had gone down in his feet, and he wanted me to come back and do more. They had tried to do the same, but they didn't seem to be able to help. Surprised that he was asking for me, I returned to continue the foot massage. Even without words there was a connective energy between us.

By Thursday my brother's family had been notified, and they were at the hospital: his wife, two sons, a daughter, Mother, and myself. The doctors did as much as they could to keep him comfortable by administering pain medications. The family got counseling from a hospital volunteer, and we chose to have a prayer conducted with the whole family while he was still alive in his hospital room. I was pleased I had a chance to tell him: "You are the most wonderful brother in the world." I am grateful to my father for honoring his true feelings by returning home. Because my father came home and my mother wanted me to return with her, I had the opportunity to travel to Phoenix and tell my brother how I felt.

On Friday, September 13, at 7 P.M., when my brother made a peaceful transition, the most amazing thing happened. We had kept the TV tuned to CNN, his favorite channel. After his passing I was unable to turn off the TV, so I turned the sound down. I must have hit another channel when I was trying to turn it off. As we were leaving his room, my niece, my mother, and I looked back at the television. There was a picture of the setting sun, and as we watched a mist appeared and a flock of birds took flight. It was a beautiful conclusion to my brother's passing. "That indicates to me that he is in peace," my mother declared. It was very reassuring to all of us.

I know it was no accident that in my search to turn off the television the relaxation channel was turned on. The peaceful presentation in that perfect moment created a beautiful memory of his passing. An intelligent force of energy had to be involved to bring us all such comfort, and I knew we are all connected.

When I came back to Los Angeles, a friend was having a party to introduce her friend's new spiritual counseling service. I attended and decided I might like to contact my brother. When the spiritual counselor asked who wanted to be first, I volunteered and followed her to the den. Just then her son entered the front door and crossed the hall in front of us. I asked who he was, and she said, "That is my son, Russ." He had the same name as my brother!

When we got to the den and sat down, she had a very important message to share with me from my brother. He wanted me to know: "I was the most wonderful sister in the world." Was it a coincidence she used the same phrase I had used with him in the hospital before he passed? Then she added, "My son just gave me a note the other day. I think it is intended for you." She went to a chest, opened a drawer and pulled out a folded piece of paper. When I unfolded it, I saw a drawing of a heart, around the heart were written the words "I love you," and it was signed, Russ. I had not told anyone what I had told my brother before he passed. Once again, I saw how we are all connected.

Electricity: the Conduit for Spirit

One month after my brother's death, in October 1996, his oldest son was getting married in Los Angeles. I asked the family to watch and see if they felt my brother's presence in some way at the wedding. A month later my older son remembered, "I noticed a burned-out light in the church ceiling over the seat where Uncle Russ would have been sitting." My sister-in-law had left an empty seat next to her. I checked the wedding photos and discovered my son was correct; the burned-out ceiling light was the one above the empty seat. I have heard that loved ones who have passed on communicate through electricity—lighting, computers, radios—even through nature.

At my father's funeral ten years later, my son again got my attention by pointing to the chandelier in the ceiling of the church. "Look, there are two burned-out lights in the only chandelier in the church," he said. We both assumed it meant my brother and father were now together.

A week after my father-in-law passed, my mother-in-law had problems with her home's electricity. It turned out all the wiring needed to be replaced in her entire home. Was it my father-in-law's way of attempting to communicate with her? I don't know, but I have witnessed many different occurrences with electricity after someone passes. I could not deny it could have been caused by the expansion of my father-in-law's non-physical energy after making his transition.

My mother enjoyed e-mailing her sister-in-law, Ida, regularly on the computer. My aunt was ninety-five years young and my mother eighty-nine. They enjoyed sharing through e-mails because my aunt lived in Nebraska, and my mother in California, limiting their ability to get together easily in person. The day before my mother received word of Aunt Ida's passing, my mother's computer failed. It turned out the entire computer, a laptop my mother had purchased less than eight months before, needed a new hard drive and had to be completely rebuilt. Fortunately, the computer was still under warranty. I can't help but think this was my aunt's way of saying goodbye to my mother.

Energy Takes Many Forms

The flight of the butterfly was a perfect example of our connection to nature and was so captivating that my older son and his fiancée could not ignore it. They were both at the hospital visiting her ill grandfather. In the courtyard outside her grandfather's window, she was on the cell phone with her grandmother, who was her father's mother and her grandfather's ex-wife. Shortly after ending her conversation, my son's fiancée had noticed a single butterfly flying around the courtyard.

This butterfly was the only one she noticed. She remembered it was very unusual, not one of the little white ones we often see, but yellow with black dots. She idly watched it fly around the courtyard in circles, then fly up to her grandfather's window, and then back around the general area where they were seated. When she turned her attention to it, the butterfly circled the area a few more times before it flew up to her grandfather's window, lingered there for a couple of seconds and then flew over the building above his room. When she went back inside, her mother said her grandfather had just passed on.

On the car ride home my son phoned me to ask what a butterfly symbolized. I often refer to the *Animal-Speak* book by Ted Andrews, a comprehensive dictionary of animal, bird, and reptile symbolism for interpretation of nature. When I looked up butterfly, it stood for "Transmutation and the Dance of Joy." That definition seemed to be quite comforting for my son and his fiancée.

After our phone call, I left to do some photocopying. While I was copying, I heard a woman behind me say, "That is much better using this paper. Now they will all fit on this size sheet." When I turned around, I was quite surprised to see she was copying sheets of butterflies. I shared with her the butterfly story. Coincidentally, the woman, Julianne, mounts butterflies and sells them at art shows. Julianne shared with me one client's story of four friends who had always done everything together. At the funeral of one, the other three reported that when they went to the cemetery to participate in the burial, they observed four butterflies dancing together on top of the coffin. We truly are one with nature, and we are all connected!

My son reported to me later that within a week of the grandfather's passing, the billboard near his fiancée's parents' home had a new advertisement. On it was a large image of butterflies with the caption, "Butterflies in Living Color."

Exercise 1:

This is a fun exercise to build your intuition, and these cards are sold in most bookstores. You will need to purchase a deck of angel cards, Zen cards, animal cards, or any deck of cards that have intuitive messages and colorful pictures. Use your cards before you meditate, or before you need to make an important decision, or just for fun. After selecting your deck of cards, find a place where you can be alone to access your own intuition and focus on the cards. Shuffle the cards while asking a question. Your question could be: *What do I need to focus on right now in my life? What do I need to be more aware of at this time*? Or just allow the information you might need to receive to come in without asking a question. Keep shuffling the cards until one just falls into your lap. It is best to read only one card at a time. If more than three cards fall out, put them back and reshuffle. If you were supposed to receive the message on those cards, it will come in again.

Part II

*

The Magic

of

Our Perspective

*

Chapter Eight
Death is not the End

As human beings, our greatness lies not so much in being able to reawaken the world but in being able to remake ourselves.
Mahatma Gandhi

While studying Feng Shui, one of my fellow colleagues gave this explanation of life and eternal energy as she held an ice cube in her hand. She said, *First the rain falls upon the earth. As the weather changes, the water freezes as in a lake that is frozen in the winter. Then in the spring the ice melts, it changes into water and then evaporates up into the sky, only to come down again in the form of rain.* We may change forms and yet our energy never disappears.

In November 1997, early in my Feng Shui career, I was referred to a woman with a delightful thirteen-year-old daughter. My client told me that at the age of two her daughter declared, "We have angels all around us." When my client asked her daughter to tell her how many angels, her daughter replied, "A cast of thousands." What makes this story unique is that the girl is now an accomplished young actress, and she was using the word "cast" at such an early age.

Could she have been an actress in a past life? Someone so young and yet so talented and accomplished at such an early age in life might definitely have an edge over other young actors if she had lived as an accomplished actress in a past life. As a child actor, losing a part to another actor may not be as devastating if one knew the other's true past before birth itself. If we keep on experiencing life after life, wouldn't it make sense that the person with the most experiences would appear to learn things more quickly in some circumstances or achieve success in certain fields with ease? On the other hand, if we don't grasp certain things very quickly, perhaps it's because the exposure to the information or experience is new in this lifetime and may have been infrequent or nonexistent in previous lifetimes.

That one reason makes it so important to avoid comparing ourselves to others. There are so many reasons why one person succeeds in certain areas and another excels in areas that are totally different. When we start comparing ourselves to others, we are defeated before we begin.

At the age of thirty, actor Matt Damon and his mother were being interviewed on a morning TV talk show. Matt's mother, Nancy, stated that Matt had acting genius in him that showed up at the age of two. "He didn't know about acting at that young age, and yet he would naturally act out skits with play figures," she said. Talent may show up at an early age as a continuation of a recent and successful past life.

Energy takes lots of different forms, but never ends. Thought is one form of energy. I feel it is possible for our thoughts to live on even after death. I also feel it is possible for those thoughts to go with us in many continuous lifetimes, becoming part of our inner spirit and energy field. I find some of my clients gravitate to certain types of period furniture. Often their craving to surround themselves with accessories or furnishings from specific historical times puzzles them. The best explanation I can offer is that their furniture represents a period in history during which they once lived. Perhaps that previous lifetime held happy memories they subconsciously want to relive.

My client with the actress daughter told me her daughter had communicated with the spirit of her uncle after he had passed. My client had often gone to visit him in the hospital during his last few days and would take her daughter, who was ten years old at the time, with her. Leaving her young daughter in the waiting room, my client would visit Dan and comfort him, wiping his brow and keeping him company. When she heard Dan had died, she was very disappointed she was not at the hospital to be with him and the family. About two weeks later my client's daughter came into her parents' bedroom in the middle of the night and was very upset, declaring there was a man in her room. Checking in the daughter's bedroom, they found nothing and put their daughter back to bed.

The next morning my client asked her daughter what the man looked like. "He wore khaki pants, an Hawaiian shirt, and a bandanna around his head like a Ninja wears," she replied. Her mother asked her what he was doing in her room, and she replied, "He kept saying 'Boo,' and he was scaring me." Later that day her mother phoned her widowed sister and asked, "What were the clothes Dan was wearing when he was buried?" Her sister answered, "A suit, why do you ask?" She told her amazed sister about the man her daughter had seen in her room. "That was Dan's favorite outfit to wear whenever he was gardening!" her sister exclaimed. She added that her two sons wanted to bury him in the gardening clothes, but she had decided on the suit. My client told her daughter the man who came to her was probably her uncle and if he came again, she should tell him she did not like him scaring her and to ask him what he wanted.

When he came again, he told the ten-year-old girl, "I want you to tell my wife how much I love her." She said to him, "I can't do that for you, you must find a way to do it yourself, and if you can't, then I may help you." Finding comfort in being with her, Dan continued to come and visit my client's daughter for about two weeks. He would be with her in the garage when she was outside working on crafts.

One day the little girl told her mother, "I am sad because Dan is leaving now, and I will miss him." She added that Dan wanted to thank her mom for the hospitality of welcoming him in her home and letting him visit. He also wanted to thank my client for wiping his brow and comforting him in the hospital. She told me, "I was surprised by the comment because my daughter did not know this and was never in the hospital room when I would visit Dan." She told her daughter to tell Dan he was always welcome in their home.

About six months went by, and one afternoon my client's sister telephoned her, telling her the strangest thing was happening. "Every time I get in my car to go anywhere, the music on the radio starts playing the same song. The lyrics of the song include this important line: 'I never told you just how much I loved you.'" My client and her daughter knew Dan had finally found a way to tell his wife he loved her. He did get what he asked for!

Losing a Father and a Diamond

In 2006, my father passed. A couple of weeks later I took my mother to a bed and breakfast in Ojai to relax for a few days. During that time we went to a beauty salon to have our nails done. After washing my hands, I sat down with the manicurist and noticed the diamond stone on my wedding ring was missing. I checked in the restroom, figuring it had fallen off when I washed my hands. I asked the owner if I could bring in a plumber to check in the drain. The owner of the salon told me she had just remolded the bathroom and did not want to take the sink apart again because she had repaired leaky pipes, and she suggested I file a claim with my homeowners insurance.

When I returned home I told my husband what had happened and he informed me he had been late renewing our house insurance and our policy had lapsed. We renewed our insurance, but I felt that claiming the stone when it had not been insured at the time would have been fraud. I did not claim my lost diamond, and I felt it was no accident I had lost my ring at that time. I created the whole event, but I did not come to realize why for another year. After the first time I lost my diamond at the weekend seminar and found it so easily, I knew if I did not find it, I must have had a reason for losing it.

Diamonds are a Girl's Best Friend

I kept asking myself why I had lost my diamond stone in a way that was so permanent. When I had lost it previously, I found it effortlessly. About a year later, another healer suggested to me I had lost my ring because my father must have been my best friend, and as people have said, "Diamonds are a girl's best friend." I had to admit I had been saying I was losing my best friend for several weeks before my father passed.

Even though what I had been saying about diamond symbols made a lot of sense, there were still issues nagging at me. The more I contemplated what had occurred before and after my father's death, the clearer it became that my history kept repeating itself.

Several months before my father passed, I had asked myself why my father was never very concerned about acquiring great wealth. Every chance he could, he donated his hard-earned money to various charities. One day, eight months before he passed, as I was relaxing and daydreaming, a vision came to me that was probably another past life.

During that past life, in the early 1900s, I was with my current parents in the private parlor car of a train. I was around ten or eleven years old. My father was very wealthy and enjoyed riding in his own private car. He wore a custom-made suit and expensive jewelry, which included a gold wristwatch, and rings on his fingers. I was sitting by the window, next to him, and my mother sat across from us. I was wearing a very smart outfit that looked like something worn by the young leading actress in the Walt Disney movie "Pollyanna." I had on a long-torso dress with a pleated skirt that was accented by a ribbon around the hip, white stockings, and patent leather button-up shoes. Around my throat was a cherished heart-shaped locket. Details about my mother were vague in this vision.

Suddenly, robbers entered our private car; their guns were drawn and pointed at my father. They asked for all his money and jewelry and my mother's as well. She gave up her wedding ring and other jewelry she had been wearing. One of the robbers grabbed the gold heart-shaped locket from my neck. Just as they turned to leave, they shot both my father and mother. I was in a state of shock. In the vision, I was taken home by the train's engineer to live with him and his family. His daughter, who was about my age, became like a sister to me.

When my father died in that past life, I made the connection between death and losing valuable jewelry. That incident explains to me why I lost my diamond within two weeks of my father's death in this life, and in a way that I could not retrieve it. I was creating from a fear of loss that I had experienced from a past life.

When we have strong emotions and add words and beliefs to that emotion, the power of creating is magnified. I am constantly being shown how we do create our reality from our thoughts, words, and emotions. So often we don't even make the connection of what we are saying and what is being created. For years I had been asleep to my feelings and emotions of the invisible energy all around us that creates our reality and can contribute to our life experiences.

I must have carried over an association of death connected with train rides into this life. In this life, my parents took me to San Diego on a train when I was fourteen. It was August 6, 1962, and the passengers, including my parents, were reading newspapers and discussing Marilyn Monroe's tragic death the day before. Although there wasn't a robbery this time, I was with my parents and I was close in age to the incident from a previous life.

Our body vibrations attract people and events to us. The more emotion is connected to an event, whether it is in this life or in a past life, the stronger the event is imbedded in our energy field. For years scientists have talked about thoughts being forms of energy, and it is clear to me that great emotion has an impact on our souls' and our bodies' energy fields, an energy that never dies.

Thoughts carried over from a past life, whether it was a memory of a traumatic event that needs to be healed, or the memory of great accomplishment that yearns for expression, may explain why you see very young children with identifiable personalities. Some children we see have great confidence, others have great curiosity, others have a fear of heights, and others enjoy being alone. Whatever experience they have just had in a past life or past lives cannot help but have some impact on the decisions and behaviors and choices they are making today. That is why we say study history, because history repeats itself.

Don't you think if we have lived before, we might repeat similar activities life after life, activities that bring us a feeling of comfort or success? Choosing something new or attempting to accomplish something different can bring fear. Fearful emotions cause us to draw what we fear to us. By letting go of our fear, life becomes more abundant, joyful, and successful. Trust and faith are major ingredients in letting go of fear.

For example, we wonder how it is that some parents tend to be very overprotective, and others tend to be more relaxed and trusting of their children. If a person had never experienced parenthood before, or had lost a child in a past life, it might cause them to be more fearful and overprotective with their current child.

It is possible that a hidden fear from a past life is within a child at birth. The fear of water or drowning, for instance, could be within the child's subconscious, just like the fear of heights, or the fear of spiders. Before birth, this child might have expressed a wish to have parents who would be protective, resulting, perhaps, in overprotective parents. According to the law of attraction, they are brought together for the learning and spiritual growth that both desire. In Asia it is common practice to study the past life of a child to increase the child's awareness of possible fears or aspirations for this lifetime. Knowing our hidden innate fears helps us overcome them consciously.

A child who had drowned in a previous life might avoid the enjoyment of water activities. I have met people who told me they have always been afraid of water and the potential for drowning, yet they could not tell me any situation in this lifetime that may have caused that fear. If what we fear, just as what we love, is attracted to us, we must focus on what we love and transform our fears into confidence.

There is nothing more painful than the loss of a child, yet a parent must realize that within a tragedy comes a new spiritual awareness for everyone who is touched by the event. Guilt is a wasted emotion and after grieving and feeling the emotional pain, letting go of any blame or guilt is the only way back to love, joy, and forgiveness.

In 2006, after my father's passing, I spent six months looking for some way my father might give me a sign that he was fine and with me in the form of energy. It happened on a warm summer night when my husband and I decided to take a ride to check my post office box. We put the top down on my convertible and we enjoyed the drive. When we arrived, my husband waited in the parking lot in the car. I approached the post office, the electronic doors opened, I walked in, and the doors closed behind me as I walked over to my P.O. Box, about twenty feet from the door.

With my back to the doors, as I began to put my key in my box, I heard the doors open behind me and then close. I thought someone was coming in behind me and didn't pause to look. Again, I heard the doors open and close behind me. I paid no attention while I opened my box. As I retrieved my mail, I heard the doors open and close again about three more times. I doubted there would be that many visitors at 11 P.M., so I turned around. There was no one there, no one was even in sight, and the doors were now closed. I locked my box, took my mail and walked toward the electronic doors.

The doors slowly opened, quite normally, and I walked through. Once outside, the doors closed behind me and I began to laugh as I walked toward the car. The doors remained closed behind me. As I got close to the car, my husband laughingly asked, "How many people did you take in with you?" The confirmation didn't come until the next day when I shared the story with my son. He said to me, "Well, of course, it was Grandpa; he retired from the post office." I realized my father was communicating with me in a way I would associate with him. He was saying hello to me from the non-physical side in a familiar setting, and I was open and ready to receive the communication he wanted to give me.

Dealing with our fears

Our thoughts create our lives, and both fear and joy attract our experiences. Strong fearful emotions result in unwanted events in our lives, and joy results in more positive experiences. Transforming our fears can be simple. Being aware of them is crucial. If you do not realize what your fears are, you are much more vulnerable than the person who is aware and can take positive action to transform that fear.

Once the fear is identified, a new positive picture or thought needs to be created in your mind to replace your fearful thought. What we strongly believe, we experience. If you do not want the feared experience, you must focus on what you do want. What we think about occurs. Yes, your thoughts are that powerful!

Once I identified a fear, I decided I would ask for what I wanted instead of allowing my fear to consume me, and in so doing, I immediately could feel the shift. It was a deep knowing that what I was now asking for replaced anything I did not want. Being clear about what you are asking for is critical. I realized all I had to do was become aware and continue to focus on what I wanted.

The gift of free will comes with a responsibility to focus on what we want in order to create our own happiness. No one can think for another. No matter how much we assist people, success comes from the individual's personal thoughts and actions. No parent can truly take credit for their child's success, anymore than they can think for the child. Success begins in our childhood with positive thoughts, and these are strengthened by positive words from parents, teachers and friends. As children mature and seek new experiences, the positive thinking they are taught to master at a young age will carry them a long way in creating future positive experiences.

Our minds are like a mini movie screen. We imagine what we want to experience, like in a movie or play, and then we get to act that script out in real life. If you constantly focus on the fear of what you do not want, your attention is very powerful and can draw that experience to you. Often, football coaches use visualization and emotion to lead their team to victory. The stronger the verbalized image, the better the movie screen becomes in our minds, and the more emotion and excitement is created. USC head football coach, Pete Carroll, uses positive thinking to lead his team to unexpected success and victories. He challenges his players to focus on positive behaviors reinforcing progress with praise.

The intensity of the emotion changes our vibration and determines how fast the desired result is experienced. The speed of the desired outcome depends on how much the desire is in alignment with the final result. Let's say you want to take a trip to Italy, and when you think about the trip you desire, you also wonder how you will be able to afford it. Your doubt splits your desire, and in turn, your vibration, which is so important to the final manifestation. You are excited to go but are apprehensive at the same time as you try to figure out how or if it will work out.

Time and time again I have discovered the process of letting go of how something will occur brings about the desire easily. Confident waiting allows the Universe to line up everything that is needed to support you on your journey. Picture yourself crossing a stream, with each step, in the moment, the rocks appear below your feet to provide the support you need to reach the other side. This is how the invisible supports you when you are in the flow, trusting, and aligned with the energy of just "letting go."

Obviously, the person who holds the strongest belief for success is the person who succeeds. If a person had experienced a past life filled with failure, it may take more effort to overcome deeply ingrained beliefs. When two people apply for the same job, the one with the strongest desire for the job, who easily sees him or herself succeeding, is the one most likely to get the job. The person who feels he or she is not up to the challenge or sees the job as boring is likely to be turned down. The release of fears before a job interview, by an encouraging parent or friend, a positive hypnotherapy session, or a counseling session, can all help to release any fears and create a successful outcome.

Society is evolving and people are learning how important it is to focus on what is wanted, enabling them to change their thinking immediately when fearful thoughts arise, and ignoring any attention to what is unwanted. In our world, life is rapidly changing and fast-paced; success or failure, and the information generated by it, can occur in the blink of an eye. This speed helps us easily see what is actually being created by our thoughts. Those who can let go of the negative and surround themselves with positive thoughts and positive people will succeed with greater ease.

Our awareness of how we are creating our lives and with whom we choose to spend time all contribute to our success. Using our imagination to create what we want is a must. Studies have shown that we use only ten percent of our mind's potential and with this realization and awareness, we have a choice to use our minds to our benefit. Becoming more intuitive, acting on our desires, and letting go of thoughts and feelings of resentment, guilt, and anger all allow room for love, joy, pleasure, and happiness. Solutions come to those who ask and are willing to take action when the idea presents itself.

Because I realize we create our own reality from our thoughts, I have learned to quickly turn a fearful thought into a more positive thought. What we think about we attract to ourselves, and we cannot hold more than one emotion at a time. Be aware of your emotions. Since joy creates a positive experience, be diligent about shifting negative emotions as quickly as possible to positive emotions. Some, myself included, have accomplished this shift by using prayer, turning the problem over to God; others identify what they don't want and focus their thinking on what they do want, while still others use affirmations to help develop positive thoughts. In all cases the act of "letting go" is the key.

Changing our thoughts to change our experiences was quickly evident to me one day when I made an unwise comment to my son's girlfriend. I told her about a family situation that concerned me. I discovered she immediately shared what I had told her with my son. I then cautioned her not to tell him everything I said because he was having a difficult and challenging time and didn't need any additional worry. "I can share anything I choose with him," she declared. Not only did she share my comment with my son, but she was so upset she didn't talk to me the rest of that day.

I realized she was right. I was being controlling but could not retrieve what I had said. Nothing I said or did that day contributed to reconciliation, until I let go. When I took a shower before bed, I visualized all negative thoughts going down the drain. I pictured a time when my son's girlfriend and our entire family had had a very connected, enjoyable, and loving time together. The next morning I received an apologetic call from her telling me how much she loved me. I saw exactly how our thoughts create our reality, both negative and positive. When I let go of the situation and pictured a happy ending, it happened.

Why do we experience the feelings of guilt, shame, blame, regret, or anger if these emotions keep us from our joy? There are numerous answers to this question. I feel, for instance, that without serious thought we accept the opinions of others and society as a whole as our own. Because of old fears, society has taught our youth to conform, and not to question authority, and in so doing young people deny their own feelings. I am noticing this attitude is changing, as many parents, teachers, and counselors receive great results by telling our teens and young adults to follow their hearts and instincts for they are the ones who truly know what's best for them. As we educate our youth and society on the importance of following our hearts and passions, many will experience more joy. When we value a person's feelings, it empowers them to become more responsible; they listen to what their heart desires and take action from true self-awareness.

To obtain true peace, we must love ourselves and respect our past choices, in this life or a previous one, without guilt. As individuals, we may go through many more experiences and even lifetimes until we can accept who we are, who we have been, and the choices we have made. Love heals, especially when we start with ourselves! Know that we can choose to recreate ourselves in every moment.

Have you noticed how many times people divorce one spouse and move on, and then end up marrying someone with a different face but the same personality and behaviors? It is important to change ourselves in order to bring in a different and improved experience. The easiest way to change is to let go of old habits and the beliefs attached to those habits.

Once we are able to identify our fears, including those hidden in our subconscious mind, we can decide on a conscious level if that fear is warranted. I believe our awareness of hidden fears is essential and once we become more aware, we can clear them almost immediately. If you feel you are not moving forward in an area of your life, I highly recommend seeking a hypnotherapist to discover what may be in your subconscious that could be sabotaging your success.

Evolution is often a slow process. It cannot be rushed: as we experience life, we receive new information and can choose again. Life is a delicious encounter of experiences to help us see and know who we really are. If you are not aware of yourself in every relationship and every experience as the one who is choosing the experience, then you are missing the greatest opportunity of all—to truly know yourself.

Exercise 1:
Without going to a hypnotherapist, sit down with a notebook and pen. Take a deep breath and relax, then take two more deep breaths and relax. Clear your mind by letting go of your thoughts. If anything comes into your mind that is distracting you from relaxing, attach that thought to the visualization of a helium balloon and allow it to float away. Concentrate on breathing in and out, and relax.

Once you're relaxed, read and answer the questions below without analyzing them. Realize and trust that your intention to receive information about an existing challenge in your life will produce clarity and the answers you need to move forward. Without judging it, write down the first answer that comes into your mind as soon as you receive the information.

Do the exercise as if you are a child playing a fun game of imagination. If it is difficult for you to believe in a past life, then picture yourself recalling a dream or a vision, or as if you are acting in a movie or play you may have seen sometime. When you are relaxed and ready, begin to read and write the answers to these questions.

1. Where is your vision taking place: what country or location?
2. Were you a male or female?
3. How old were you?
4. What were you wearing?
5. When you are satisfied with that image, move to an important event in that life.

6. Write about that event, giving as much detail as you can.

7. How do you make a living in that life? Or is there something specific you do everyday?

8. Who were the other people in your life?

9. Imagine yourself in various events of that life where you felt sad or upset and describe that occasion or event.

10. Take as long as you need write everything down.

11. Write about a joyful time in that life.

12. If there is anything else you need to know about that experience, write it down.

13. Advance to the time when you died and describe that moment. Was it quick? Were you in a place of your choosing? Who was with you at the time?

14. Picture yourself passing and in a peaceful place. What did you learn from that life and those experiences? What would you like to change about that life if you could? What was the one thing you learned from that life?

15. See if anything you wrote is similar to the life you are living now. Are your beliefs related to anything in this past life vision?

16. Did you gain any new understanding about the choices you are making today?

Chapter Nine
The Energy of Past Lives

The mind once enlightened cannot again become dark.
Thomas Paine, *Common Sense*

The synchronicities now seemed to be appearing more often. The more I asked and let go, the more people and events and guidance would show up in my life unexpectedly. As I continued to ask questions, answers would follow the question with unexpected events showing up in synchronistic ways. People would show up in my life to give me support, answers would come through songs on the radio, or by opening a page of a book at a bookstore. Even TV shows would carry strong messages to give me the answers I was seeking. I was surprised to see how easily the answers appeared after I asked.

Not long ago I recuperated from a cold, which really hit me hard. It surprised me to have any health issues because I had avoided the seasonal flu for several years. When I asked why this had occurred, the answer came almost immediately: *You have not been receiving enough lately. You need to say yes when offered support. Be more aware of receiving. Nurture yourself more.* As I pondered the answer, the phone rang. My husband's cousin, Linda, who owns a salon that specializes in body and facial services, was calling to treat me to a cranial massage and a lymphatic drain treatment. I had never experienced either before, and I knew she was sent to me by the Universe, because the call came in so quickly after I received the message. I immediately accepted and had a very relaxing session—just what I needed.

In 1995, I began focusing on prevention and being proactive to create good health. Our health is a reflection of our inner feelings and beliefs. I started with a nutritionist to clean the body of toxins, went on to clear allergies, joined a gym and hired a personal trainer. I began learning everything I could about natural methods to help clear blocks and to build a strong immune system by drinking pure water, breathing clean air, and enjoying deep sleep. Loving yourself is demonstrated when you support and nurture your body, mind, and spirit.

When I first started to learn more about alternative health options, I was waiting for my chiropractic appointment. I met an interesting woman there and when I explained Feng Shui to her briefly, she told me she could teach me how to do muscle testing. We planned to exchange services.

She phoned me about a week later. After talking a short time, she informed me she detected from my voice that I had many allergies, but none of them seemed to be food related, which was quite unusual. She told me studies have shown that people who have allergic reactions to pollens, etc., usually have food allergies as well. I mentioned I had spent a lot of time working on my health, and went regularly to an allergy clinic where a special dose of ingredients was prepared by computer in exact proportions based on the foods my body reacted to most.

Diamonds Keep Reappearing

Over a period of nine months, I periodically received a small bottle of allergens by mail for self-injected shots to build up my resistance. "Obviously, it worked!" she declared. I was quite surprised she could detect my positive results based on her analysis of my voice. "Did you know you were a diamond thief in a past life?" she suddenly commented. I was stunned, and had to admit that could have been a possibility, because I was having so many experiences concerning diamonds.

I hadn't given much thought about the possibility of past lives at that time. How she came up with a diamond thief was puzzling to me. Had I been wondering on a subconscious level why diamonds kept coming up for me? I didn't yet realize this question would have an answer; I was still unaware of the power of asking in order to receive information and support.

Coincidentally, shortly afterward, a good friend and certified hypnotherapist offered to give me a hypnotherapy session. Uninformed, I hesitated because I felt hypnosis would give someone else control over my mind. I learned all hypnosis is self-hypnosis, and the therapist is only a guide to help you focus. In reality, because you are more focused and aware, you are more in control in hypnosis than out of it. Hypnosis, my friend explained, helps relax the subject so they can get past the conscious resistant mind and others' opinions to connect with the subconscious mind.

With my hesitation came a nudge from the Universe. I kept meeting hypnotherapists everywhere I went. Another friend declared, "I think the Universe is trying to tell you something. Maybe you should take her up on her offer." I agreed and afterward, my hypnotherapist friend told me I might be processing information for a few days.

I was unloading my dishwasher the day after my session, allowing my imagination to wander, when suddenly I started crying. I wondered what it was about as I pictured myself at a church orphanage surrounded by children. Why was I so sad? I was a single woman who had gotten pregnant after being attacked and had been brought to a church to live until delivering my child.

I was giving my newly delivered child away to a woman who couldn't have children. I felt the pain of that moment. Is this woman in my life now? I asked myself. The answer was astonishing: that woman is my mother now. She couldn't have children in her past life, and I realized why I have often remarked that my current mother loves babies so much she would have enjoyed having ten children. Now it makes more sense to me why I have always felt that way about her.

I was surprised how realistic everything in that past life seemed. My present husband was a priest in that life and served at the church where I stayed until I gave birth. I fell in love with him then, but he felt obligated to honor his commitment to the church. It all made sense in a strange way why we came together in this life.

Even now my husband listens attentively, just like a priest. In this life he chose to be a firefighter and served as a fire captain in an atmosphere of mostly men. Maintaining a firehouse has many similarities to a church, and his career in this life also focused on saving lives.

I continued to recall the past life and saw myself after giving up my child. Afterward, I went to live with a woman I met through the church, an interior designer by trade. She taught me a great deal about design, I became her assistant, and she helped me start a new life.

I met that woman in my present life, and I immediately knew instinctively I had known her before. A very good friend in this life, although I haven't known her a long time, she is the one who suggested I take up my friend's offer for hypnotherapy. At a time when I was looking for answers, she helped me put the puzzle together. I find it humorous how her talent for decorating from the past life shows up in her own home and in everything she does. Her attention to detail in that past life as a designer is probably what led her to a career in engineering in this life!

In my present life, I think it's funny that I loved to rearrange furniture from a very young age. My first experience came when I was eight years old and I stayed overnight at a friend's home. I asked my friend if we could sneak into her parents' living room and rearrange their furniture during the middle of the night. She agreed, and we went downstairs where we moved a sleek seven-foot sofa, and then grouped end tables and armchairs around the sofa. We had a great time together and I felt good about the new floor plan.

When we got up the next morning, we were greeted in the living room by her mother, who didn't seem as pleased as we were to have her living room transformed. She didn't make us put it back, but I knew after I left it would be put back the way it had been. I can't remember being invited back to spend the night again, but shortly afterward my family moved to California.

Since I enjoy decorating, I majored in art in college and by the time I was thirty-two I had started my own interior design firm. I taught interior design at a local college, giving others an opportunity, as I had been given, to have a creative career. I had been asked several times by design students I studied with in college how I could start my own interior design business right out of college without working for another designer or established design firm.

It makes sense to me now that if I had worked as an assistant to a designer in a past life, starting my own design business in this life was just the next step. After this past life regression it all made sense to me why I had chosen to do things that I have done in my life today. I went on to have numerous past life regressions after the impact this first one had on my life. The past life regressions have helped me to better understand who I am, and why I like the things I do.

I found my much resisted hypnotherapy session very enlightening. Had I been more aware of my past life sooner, I wonder how it might have impacted my present life. Everything always unfolds in perfect timing. As society evolves, I believe people will become more aware of their past lives in order to understand their talents and to clear their fears so they can enjoy a joyful present life, which comes with a high vibration of love. It's all part of our journey, which cannot be rushed, but allowed to unfold according to events and the choices we make.

The choice to let go and do the right thing for my child, for the woman who wanted children, and to support myself during that past life, resulted in huge gains for everyone, which continued into my present life. I believe I drew from my previous skills of design to create a career with flexible hours, allowing me to focus on my most important value in this life: my children and family. Having my own business allowed me to control the number of clients I worked with and the hours I would spend, thus I was able to put my children first in this lifetime, which was something I longed for in my past life. Having a belief in past lives gives us the opportunity to strive to do our best now, and also to lighten up, knowing this is not the end. We are all made of energy, and energy never dies, it just changes form.

As my hypnotherapist friend indicated, I would be processing information for several days and I should just allow it to happen. As I processed these "memories," I began to realize that I chose to give up my child because I was a single mother who did not have enough money to properly support her child. That past life helped me understand why I put the highest value on my children and family today. It has also helped me to understand the plight of women and their responsibility to make difficult choices that relate to bearing children. It certainly has made me more understanding.

Hypnotherapy was just one tool I used to understand more fully who I am.

It is said that history repeats itself. I know from experience that we continue to repeat actions, even though we know we want things to be different. It is really important to change ourselves in order to change life patterns and experiences. I know now I need to know myself so I may choose actions that support who I am. I believe we are here on earth to learn how to love and to forgive, not only others, but ourselves as well: to let go of guilt and regrets, and to grow and enjoy new experiences. Life is what we choose it to be.

If your beliefs are contradictory to your desires, you will get what you believe, not what you desire. Consequently, it's vitally important to understand your beliefs. Beliefs are created when we are young and hear adults share their beliefs; they come from our experiences growing up with friends, and from our school days. Beliefs are acquired and discarded during our entire lives, inevitably becoming part of a past life.

Once I experienced a hypnotherapy past life regression, I realized my hesitation toward the initial experience was keeping me from becoming more aware. Once I discovered the benefits from the experience, I was able to let go of any further fear or resistance. I began to choose the experience of a past life regression anytime I felt I was not moving forward in my life. I could see how my actions in past lives affected what was happening in my life at the time. Before a session, I always asked to be taken to a time in this life or another that might be influencing my progress at that moment.

What made me a believer of past life regression therapy was how fast results would occur after a session. I had been working part-time for a company that used advancement in rank for their business associates as a way of recognizing people as they attained success with the company. These rank advancements were named after stones and precious metals: Silver, Gold, Platinum, Diamond, and Royal Diamond. At one point, I had successfully reached the Silver level but was having a challenge reaching the level of Gold.

I followed all the suggestions to increase business from those above me in rank. Nothing seemed to be working. I chose to have a hypnotherapy session and had a vision of a ship similar to Disneyland's pirate ships. I saw rows of gold bricks on the bottom of the ship: gold that had been payment for cargo that my partner and I had recently delivered. We were returning home with our payment when my partner woke me up one night with a gun pointing at my head. He forced me onto a small boat, took me to a nearby island and dropped me off. While my deceitful partner sailed home with the gold, I was left to die.

So that was why I didn't want to go for the Gold rank! With a memory of death associated with gold, it was no wonder I was avoiding it at any cost. The session took place on a Thursday. On Saturday I spoke on Feng Shui at a women's conference and invited participants from the seminar to visit my home the following Monday evening for a demonstration from the company whose products I represented.

Six women attended the presentation, and a few days later several returned for more information. Within three weeks two people had joined the company and quickly advanced to the Silver level, along with one of my previous associates who also reached Silver. I reached the Gold level in a matter of weeks and had done nothing differently than before to explain this rapid achievement, except for the hypnotherapy past life regression.

Was I putting out a vibration that sent a different message than before, thereby attracting what I no longer feared? After spending the past five years attempting to go from Silver to Gold, I was astounded I advanced to Gold immediately and to the Platinum level in just six months, and to top it off won a trip to Japan for my husband and me.

The hypnotherapy session, whether it was real or not, made sense to me about certain feelings and choices I have made in this life. I do not believe that past life was a creation of my imagination, especially because of the timing of the information. When I let go of the fear of experiencing the unknown, my strong desire to move forward helped the solution to appear. As we ask, we receive the answers if we are open and willing to listen and receive.

Our life is filled with choices. When we know what we want and ask for it, the law of attraction brings a corresponding energy to us in the form of people, events, or things. Whether we are able to receive the good we want is based on our inner beliefs about ourselves. If we carry guilt, fear, anger, resentment, it is much more difficult to let the good in.

Negative emotions stand in the way of our love for ourselves and block the good we deserve.

I discovered Feng Shui at a perfect time in my life when I was asking for a new passion. If our physical body dies and transforms into earth, or dust, what happens to our energy field? Do we carry memories of our life with us in our energy field? That energy field exists in the non-physical until we have a desire to be in a physical body again. For me, it explains how children are so talented they can express themselves as great musicians or artists at a very young age with no formal training. I believe before our birth we choose to be who we want to be and experience what we desire in our upcoming life.

I saw the Academy Award winning movie, "The Queen" and a week later, "Marie Antoinette." After watching both movies, I imagined that Marie Antoinette could have come back in this life as Princess Di, which occurred to me because Princess Di was referred to as the People's Princess. During the French Revolution, the people imprisoned the unloved Marie Antoinette with her children and she was eventually guillotined. When we die in a traumatic way, like she did, it could create a strong desire to create the opposite in another lifetime.

Ask and you shall receive. Some may refer to this as karma, but I feel it is our choice to experience whatever we choose in each physical life experience, having an opportunity to make what we felt was a negative into a positive. It balances our non-physical energy, and allows us to learn and grow. Some say we have a life review after our death to decide if we are pleased with the choices we've made in the life we have just completed. Not being judged by God, we become our own judges, causing God to represent the ultimate loving and allowing non-physical energy. This view puts the responsibility for our lives back on us, and allows us to decide if we are pleased or if we would like to come again and experience similar situations, making different choices to have different outcomes, thus allowing greater wisdom.

Letting go of a decision that is running us on a subconscious level changes our life immediately. Being open-minded to various methods of healing that could help us let go shifts our consciousness, gaining a new awareness. It is our experiences that allow us to grow and gain wisdom. Mistakes have been embraced by the most successful people in the world. If you were to embrace your failures without judgment, wouldn't that help you to be more allowing, loving and at peace with yourself and others? It is our thoughts about ourselves that make us fearful and anxious. Change the thought and with great amazement your life will change as well.

In order to have a joyful life, letting go of judgment about yourself and others works magic. It is really that simple, and the awareness of any limiting beliefs that can be brought to the surface by a past life will be put in perspective when we realize we are living in a different time and with different circumstances.

Giving ourselves the understanding of how that was then, and this is now gives us the ability to choose again. Don't allow yourself to react from a feeling deep inside that makes no sense to you and is hidden from your conscious awareness. Do whatever it takes for you to learn the truth about your beliefs, love yourself enough to investigate and understand the belief. By identifying the belief, it can be easily released. Finding the truth about our beliefs is simple. Today, there are many natural healing therapists who work to help people discover their limiting beliefs so they can let go of beliefs that may be holding them back from their success and happiness. I believe it is absolutely essential that we become aware. The people of the world are waking up. Rapidly changing technologies have helped us to expand our awareness.

Presidential Similarities

When I began to study our political candidates closely during our 2008 U.S. elections, I began to see many similarities between Barack Obama and Abraham Lincoln. I believe Obama might have been Lincoln in a past life because of the parallels in their lives. Obama and Lincoln are both tall and thin. They both have large ears, symbolizing their desire to listen to the people. Lincoln was concerned for equality for all people and fought to free the slaves. Obama similarly believes in hope for all people. If Lincoln did choose to come back now to make this point for equality, he may have chosen to be a racially mixed person to exemplify his belief that all races are equal.

Lincoln was depressed about the Civil War and how it divided our nation during his presidency. Obama talks a great deal about his concern to negotiate first before starting a war. We have seen Obama's gift for speaking, which would come easily to an experienced President from the past. Other similarities: Obama was the senator from Illinois, and also held his first campaign move to announce his bid for President in Springfield, Illinois, the state's capitol when Abraham Lincoln was President.

In Obama's first speech to open his campaign, he used words that could have easily been spoken by President Lincoln at the end of the Civil War. Obama was quoted by the Associated Press, February 10, 2007, when he announced he was seeking the Democratic nomination for President in 2008: "In the face of war, you believe there can be peace. In the face of despair, you believe there can be hope. In the face of a politics that's shut you out, that's told you to settle, that's divided us for too long, you believe we can be one people, reaching for what's possible, building that more perfect union."

Sounds like a speech Abraham Lincoln would have made referring to our union of states. Recently, Abraham Lincoln has been applauded for his ability to write. Literary historian, Fred Kaplan, has been quoted as saying, "Lincoln belongs among literary giants." Obama in similar character has been credited for his excellence in authoring his own book, *The Audacity of Hope*.

Lincoln won re-election in 1864. Planning for peace, the President was flexible and generous, encouraging Southerners to lay down their arms and join in reunion. Lincoln's Second Inaugural Address is now inscribed on the wall of the Lincoln

Memorial in Washington, D.C. "With malice toward none, with charity for all, with firmness in the right, as God gives us to see the right, let us strive on to finish the work we are in, to bind up the nation's wounds..." On Good Friday, April 14, 1865, Lincoln was assassinated at Ford's Theatre in Washington. With Lincoln's death, the possibility of peace with magnanimity died. Maybe what Lincoln committed to at the time of his death was to come back and live a life where he could finish his desire for the possibility of achieving peace.

As new President-elect Obama and his wife Michelle toured the White House with President Bush and his wife Laura, Obama was quoted saying, "It just doesn't seem right to have a flat screen TV in the Lincoln bedroom." Who would have been most concerned about what happened in the Lincoln bedroom? I would think Lincoln himself would be the one to have such a thought, or someone who was very close to him.

After being elected to the office of President, and before taking office, on November 16, 2008, Barack Obama was interviewed by Steve Kroft, *60 Minutes* TV correspondent. Obama was asked what he was reading to prepare for his new position as President. He replied, "I've been spending a lot of time reading Lincoln...there is a wisdom there and a humility about his approach to government, even before he was President, that I just find very helpful." Kroft commented, "He put a lot of his political enemies in his cabinet." Obama replied, "He did." Then Kroft asked, "Is that something you're considering?" Obama answered, "Well, I tell you what. I find him (Lincoln) a very wise man."

Los Angeles CBS news anchorwoman, Sharon Tay, reported on January 10, 2009, that for his inauguration on January 20 as the 44th U.S. President, Barack Obama will be using the same bible Lincoln used when he was sworn in on March 4, 1861. With so many parallels between the personalities of Obama and Lincoln, one cannot help but conclude that Obama could have been President Lincoln in a past life.

A belief in past lives has helped me solve questions about unexplainable fears, desires that drive people with unstoppable determination, and why we sometimes have experiences we say we do not want. One primary example: my reluctance and apprehension to start organizing and writing this book. To obtain clarity on the situation, I chose to listen to a CD with a guided meditation that took me into a past life regression.

When I got comfortable and began to listen to the guided meditation, in my mind I saw a man sitting at an old desk in a dimly lit room. The room was circular, as seen in the turrets of France and the walls were made of gray cement block. The room was very stark, and the man appeared to be rather isolated. It could have been a room in a prison tower or in a castle during the 16th century in France. The man wore a clean white shirt with long sleeves and tight trousers and what appeared to be riding boots. It was unclear to me where this room was located. I know little about the actual building. It looked like a quiet place and he appeared to be writing a book with a quill pen and a bottle of ink.

The meditation suggested I advance my mind to an important event. I observed that same man walking down a street filled with quaint small shops as seen along the sidewalks in France during the 16th century. The man stopped in front of a bookstore window and seemed to be staring inside the window at a book. *What was so important about this book?* I asked myself. I received the message this man had written the book, someone had plagiarized it, a large publisher had printed it, and the fake author's book was the one featured in the window. Word for word it was the same story.

I knew right away I was the man who had originally written that book. No wonder I didn't want to put forth my efforts to write another book! I had feared that my work would be in vain and it would be copied again. My underlying fear was creating my paralyzed action to begin working on my current book. Once the reason for my delay was revealed to me, I was able to write with passion and enthusiasm to complete this book.

Amazingly, it also explained an actual event from twenty years ago in my present life. When my sons were younger, I partnered with another parent and we co-authored a book for swimmers to track their personal swim times at competitive swim meets. It became a very popular book with swimmers and swim teams. Not long after our book came out, a major company that carried swim products introduced a new recordkeeping book for swimmers, and I discovered they had created the exact copy of our book.

A lawyer told my partner and me that, since our book had been copyrighted, the swim company had committed a Federal offense. "They copied every page using your book as camera-ready art," the lawyer laughed. The suit would cost us $17,000 because we needed a Federal Marshall to gather up all the books they had in stock, and they would not be able to sell the books until a court hearing was held. Since our books were selling for only $4.95 and had been created to benefit swimmers, and our own children, we decided not to sue.

We dissolved our partnership and sold all rights to print and sell our book to another swim team parent. I can see that I created this copyright theft several years before because I was subconsciously acting from a place of fear based on events in a past life. And I was still afraid my work would be copied and I might experience betrayal or robbery again. Since we create everything we experience in our lives, this past life regression explained how I could have brought this experience into my life. Historians study how history repeats itself; with this example we see how history could carry over from one lifetime to the next through our emotions.

Exercise 1:

I suggest you consider a session with a hypnotherapist; it need not be one to explore past lives. You may find it very relaxing and helpful for any area of your life causing you some challenges. Another suggestion is to purchase a recording to do your own independent guided hypnosis. I have found Dick Sutphen's "Past Life Regression" CD to be very beneficial, but you may choose to do your own exploring on the Internet.

Chapter Ten
What's in Your DNA?

There is nothing wrong for a man to fear, but there is something wrong for a man to allow fear to control his life.
Author Unknown

If you are having challenges accepting the theory of past lives, consider another method that may explain how we have developed our present beliefs. This idea may be more comfortable and in alignment with your present beliefs, and could help you better understand who you are, and enable you to easily let go of beliefs that no longer serve you. Letting go of beliefs that hold you back is the goal of my entire book. Trusting your own intuition, realizing and accepting your greatness, as well as enjoying more of your desires and preferences are what make life extraordinary. How you choose to discover is up to you. Remember: **It is not the method; it is the message that is most important.**

This quote came when I was attending a weekly meeting for women held by a marriage and family counselor. It was a great group of six women who were on a journey of self-discovery. I brought a recent self-help book I was reading to share with the group and in it were suggestions of steps to take to improve your life.

One woman in the group began to press me for an answer about which step needed to be taken first. I was puzzled: to me the book had the spiritual message to allow your intuition to speak to you using the various steps suggested in order to discover who you are. This woman was caught up in wanting a step-by-step structured outline in order to have the success she desired. It was as if there were only one perfect method to accomplish her desire, and she wanted desperately to find that one magic method.

On my drive home, I asked God how I could best answer her, and the divinely inspired message that came to me was: *It's not the method, it's the message.* Short and to the point, those few words convey amazing wisdom for our lives. That message helped me realize I could not answer that for her.

What feels right is the best step to take, and feelings are personal. No one can feel what you are feeling in any given moment. No one can ever deny what you are feeling. When we allow and accept our feelings to give us feedback, then we gain the important message about our beliefs. If we are able to question those beliefs, we can let go of the ones that no longer serve us and move forward on our own spiritual journey of loving and allowing. Every time we think we have the answer for someone else, or the perfect method to help solve another's problem, I remember: *It's not the method, it's the message.*

This quote has been demonstrated often for me. In my journey to experience new methods to release the old, detoxify the body, improve my mind or just enjoy a pampering and relaxing afternoon enjoying a new method to move the Chi in my body, mind and spirit, what I would often hear the practitioner say in their passion to help their client, "This is the best method to help the client clear old habits or outdated beliefs." A better statement would be, "This is the best method the practitioner has found to help their client." No one knows what the best method for the client will be until the client has the experience.

I feel the same goes for religions. Even though I was raised with the teachings of Jesus, I now understand that those who have studied the teachings of Buddha, Mohamed, or any other teacher who has come in to teach God's love, helps people by their message, and the method is irrelevant. Wars have occurred over what is the right method to honor God, and yet if God stands for loving and allowing, those who allow others their message are in alignment with God and are practicing the art of letting go.

What if you received your beliefs through your DNA, having energy and vibrations of certain beliefs being passed on at birth from one generation to another? This could explain how people, during hypnotherapy, recall a life that can be traced back to an actual person who lived during the time they experience while under hypnosis.

It is possible that we carry undetected memories of our ancestors' lives with us in our DNA. If doctors investigate our potential for diseases based on our family history, then why wouldn't we also carry the potential for life successes, fears, and beliefs in our DNA?

A few days after I began writing this chapter, I saw a television documentary about two male scientists working on a theory that our ancestors' memories are passed on through DNA. I did not catch the name of these two men, but as I started to do more research, I discovered that other scientists are just beginning to take notice of their theory, studies are being done on their documentations, and more and more research is being conducted to support their studies. Their studies focus on the question: Is it possible to access other ancestral memories located in our DNA? Could their studies reveal an explanation for past-life regression? Scientists are now asking, "When clients regress to memories from previous lives, is it actually them accessing something present in their genome blueprint, an ancestral experience?"

As I did further research I found that neurobiologist Sandra Pena de Ortiz suggests that somehow the brain must retain an archived blueprint of each neural network in order to create the replacement neuron as a structural and functional clone of its predecessor. Some scientists go even further and suggest that these memory molecules might store information themselves, that each individual neuron contains memory.

Did I receive this information from the Universe? It certainly reinforced for me that I am connected by thought to others and it shows how the law of attraction is always working. When we are on the same thought pattern as others, we are attracted to them, according to our thought vibrations. The fact that I saw my idea on TV two days after I wrote about it was no accident.

When Oprah Winfrey, the television host, had her family genealogy traced, she learned an ancestral grandfather had started a school for black children. To Oprah, this fact explained why she had a burning desire to start a school for young black girls. Believing in DNA memories being passed from one generation to the next in our cells and subconscious helps confirm Oprah's passion.

Be aware of your thoughts and what you are focusing on since our thoughts carry vibrations, and there is the potential for positive or negative results because of them. Realizing and effectively clearing negative thoughts or beliefs contribute to raising our body's energy vibration. It allows us to go with the flow and to eliminate frustration as we move forward with our new goals. By keeping your focus on positive thoughts and desires, your life experiences become positive as well.

If you look at what you have in life, you'll always have more. If you look at what you don't have in life, you'll never have enough. Oprah Winfrey, Television Host, Actress and Producer

Being satisfied, being comfortable in your environment and your position in society, may contribute to your reluctance to let go of the old that no longer serves you. Your comfort level may prevent you from embracing any new thought or behavior, or allow you new choices. You may find that if you do not **let** go, the Universe will step in to assist you in letting go, and the process may not be as comfortable as it might have been had you initiated it.

Christine's story

As I was writing this book, my friend Christine shared a wonderful story about her experience with letting go and how her ego almost kept her from one of the most treasured times in her life. She told me that when she was growing up, her mother was her definition of strength. Her father had passed away when she was ten, and her mother had to raise five children alone. Her sister, the youngest, was only five months old at the time, and their economic status dropped from upper-middle class to just above poverty level, until her mother completed college and went into her full-time career several years later.

It was a very difficult transition for all of them. Because her mother, who had never worked, went back to college to get her degree in social work, Christine acquired responsibilities beyond her youthful capabilities. The effort of keeping the family together in their home made them very close, however.

Despite Christine's closeness with her mother, she told me she felt she had made a strange decision not to be by her mother's side during the last weeks of her life. Perhaps, Christine recalled, she was thinking her new job at the FAA's National Operations Command Center in Washington, DC, was too important.

She had been hired for a special project after the September 11 terrorist attacks and was quickly offered a permanent job, which would include a transfer for her husband as well. Even though her intuition indicated the job was not the right deal for her, her ego wanted it.

The problems started right from the beginning with the "move from hell," Christine said, and ended with discovering the supervisor had lied about getting her husband relocated. The decline and downward spiral of her life began then, and it didn't take long for her to see just how unimportant her job was. She felt she was attracting bad luck in every aspect of her life, from car problems to friction with friends and co-workers. Because of her unhappiness, she began having physical challenges. First she broke out in boils around her neck after a heated discussion with her supervisor, then her chest began to feel tight and she feared she might have a heart attack. Her husband expressed concern that she would "lose it."

While all this was happening, Christine explained, she was struggling with her plans to take time off from her career to be with her mother. Her mind instead of her heart was dominating as she debated about when to go to her mother and how much time she would need.

Christine told me her loving husband could see more clearly than she could and suggested they both take a month off to visit her mother. She would have an opportunity to get away and get back to herself while also spending the time with her dying mother. Christine and her husband packed up the RV and drove from Virginia to Idaho, and she told me with heartfelt joy that the month ended up being one of the greatest gifts of her life. Christine and her mother rekindled the special bond they had when she was younger, which had faded a bit with distance and her adult independence.

Christine had been told once that the last thing we learn from our parents is how to die. She told me she had been blessed with an amazingly strong and insightful mother. Because Christine was finally willing to let go and allow the Universe to speak to her loudly and clearly that she needed to be with her mother, Christine was blessed to see and experience her mother's strength again, which began the healing process of her own soul.

Christine expressed to me that she fully believes the chaotic events that had occurred after taking the job in Virginia were Divine Guidance. She knew she could have made the choice to be there for her mother many times before she finally let go and went to be with her. "I had made other choices I thought would serve me better. I realize now that those choices only served my ego."

Shortly after her mother's death, Christine gave birth to the child she and her husband thought they would never be able to conceive. She quit the job she had started to hate and rekindled her passion! Christine concluded, "In letting go, I allowed my mother to give birth to me once again!"

Unwanted Fears

Awareness of unwanted fears you may be carrying within the cells of your body and mind can help to increase your clarity. Clarity, in turn, allows you to choose a career, relationships, social activities, and experiences that will bring you joy. Feelings of joy bring positive results.

There is nothing wrong for a man to fear, but there is something wrong for a man to allow fear to control his life, an American soldier recently said, quoting his father. We have free will and are responsible for our choices in what we experience. Often our choices are made at a deep subconscious level, without our conscious awareness, and create results that negate our joy, leaving us puzzled and perplexed. "If we create our reality, then why would I purposefully create a negative result?" you ask. Negative results come from negative hidden fears. Discover your hidden fears and let go once and for all.

Studies have shown that when we cleanse and detoxify our body by first letting go of toxins, we can effectively release excess pounds and achieve our weight goal much easier. What if we have toxic ancestral memories in our DNA keeping us stuck in a state of fear or anxiety, or, in the opposite case, a positive desire driving us to success and remarkable achievement?

Psychologists have found that our environments have a tremendous effect on our success. In Christine's case, did her early life in poverty and struggle influence her decision to stay at the job, even though her heart wanted to leave? Or could it have been a strong feeling of responsibility attracted to her in childhood, responsibilities carried over from a past life? The child who has supportive parents and other encouraging adults in the family, along with a clean and structured environment, tends to achieve success more easily than those who have lived with poverty, abuse, and a lack of parental guidance, unless they have taken on another's unwarranted fears, or have a DNA or past life influence.

There are those who overcome their negative environments, which have spurred them on to great success rather than acting as a deterrent to their desires, much like Christine, who continues to succeed professionally. Becoming aware, clear, and passionate about your dreams and focusing on your vision without distraction is one way to accomplish a magical life. Do what it takes to focus on your passion, and if you need to let go of any negative thoughts, make that your first step, trusting and allowing your heart to lead.

If you have grown up with a parent who carries a strong fear, such as a fear of spiders, you may have unknowingly taken on that fear when you were a child. Awareness of your own feelings is the key to releasing any unwarranted fears you may hold. Letting go of a fear is as simple as making a decision to go forward and leave behind that which no longer serves you. When you are moving in the direction of your passion, the letting go becomes easier.

If, in a past life, you were bitten by a spider and died, that traumatic death may have imprinted your thoughts or DNA. Thus you would probably avoid all spiders in the future and may have created an unwarranted fear in this life. When we lose touch with our true feelings, and react from the ego to people or life situations, our DNA, past life history, early childhood environment, or any other person or situation may be causing an unnatural influence over our hearts. We may then attract a situation that will get our attention, just like it did for Christine.

If there is too much fear and a strong lack of confidence about succeeding, you are giving into what you fear and sabotaging your own efforts, which keeps you from taking the next step to receive the experience you so strongly desire. It can be a vicious cycle when a person almost reaches success and then something happens to keep them from succeeding. When this happens over and over again, it is clear that something is blocking their move forward to achieve their true desire. There are so many supportive alternatives that can help us let go. Some examples of these various practices are: Hypnotherapy, NLP (Neurolinguistic Programming), Chakra Balancing, Acupuncture, Chiropractic, Cranial Massage, Body Massage, Feng Shui, Reiki, Holographic Breathing Therapy, Theta Healing, and other mind and body practices that help clear toxins and raise our energy vibration to achieve success easily. Thinking that letting go has to be difficult is an outdated belief, and when changed helps your life unfold effortlessly.

Applying the law of attraction is as simple as being aware of your thoughts. Let go of any negativity that arises and replace negative thoughts with positive ones. Pick something you have enjoyed and when a negative thought arises, focus on the positive experience. As we focus on the positive, the negative events in our lives will slowly disappear.

Always ask yourself if you are remembering a troublesome past experience or if you are focusing on the present moment.

When it involves something from the past, the only way to enjoy the moment and have peace of mind is to let go of the thought from the past, whether it is a memory of a childhood experience, or a past life trauma. Identifying thoughts based on a past life are the easiest to release because we know it has nothing to do with our present reality. If we continue to believe in our contradictory feelings, we are living an illusion.

This quote by Og Mandino eloquently reinforces the importance of our thoughts. *I will waste not even a precious second today in anger or hate or jealousy or selfishness. I know that the seeds I sow I will harvest, because every action, good or bad, is always followed by an equal reaction. I will plant only good seeds this day.* Og Mandino 1923-1996, Author and Speaker.

Our thoughts are prayers

Society tells us it is noble to fight against those things we do not want in our lives like cancer, drugs, crime, etc. Take the example of the war against cancer: millions have been spent in finding a cure and demonstrations organized against the disease, and yet we have more cases of cancer in our society today than ever before. Too little effort has been directed to embrace positive choices with thoughts about improved health, prevention, and vitality rather than focusing on the disease.

If what we resist persists, then "wars" against cancer, drugs and the like don't work. We must let go of the fight. Think about what we desire instead. If we concentrate on the disease, for instance, our mind helps to strengthen the negative. Distracting ourselves with happy thoughts helps our body revert to its natural state of wellness. It really is simple, and yet so many want to make it hard.

People often talk about their illness as a way to get attention. The person with the most challenging story related to their disease is often the one who gets the most sympathy and compassion from others. If we realize the best help we can give the ill is to focus on an expectation for their good health and improvement of their lives, we can avoid discussing the negative aspects and instead be supportive in positive ways.

I visited a man who'd broken his hip and was in the hospital. When I arrived, his family was gathered around him looking very sad, and whispering about how ill he was. I was surprised to see the nurse on duty was the wife of my husband's best friend. I privately asked, "Could you tell me about his condition? Is he close to death?" When she studied his chart, she told me he appeared fine.

The next day we got a call that he had passed while at the physical therapy center where they had taken him. I asked a minister friend why he had died when he had seemed well. She told me if someone does not care about the outcome of their own fate, others sending fear-based thoughts may impact that person's life. And he could have gotten caught up in his own belief that if he had broken his hip, he would not be able to recover and have the same quality of life. He apparently made a quiet transition; once alone and away from loved ones, he was able to make his transition easier than in their presence. Every moment of our lives we are responsible for our experiences, even in death.

My friend Donna and I love to have spiritual discussions of the meaning of life. After the death of my husband's good friend, Kirk, in the September 1978 PSA plane crash, she told me she felt we have contracts before we come into our lives. We play specific roles so we can interact with others to create certain experiences for our personal growth. "Even by our choice of death, we have made an agreement with those we love," she said but did not feel anything was set in stone. She explained to me, "It is like you get a nudge from the Universe stating, 'OK, do you remember what you decided before you were born and the agreements you made with loved ones to help their growth? Do you still want to be on the plane that will crash?" She added, "If the person changes their mind at the last minute, it is OK since every moment is our choice and the privilege of free will."

My husband and I learned that the day before Kirk was to board the plane he was hesitant and had told my husband's brother that he did not want to travel, even though it was a short plane trip for business from Los Angeles to San Diego. We also learned that his only brother was scheduled to be on the same plane, and at the last minute had canceled his flight.

Transform Your Life with Comedy

When Norman Cousins, former editor of "The Saturday Review," returned from a trip to the Soviet Union in 1964 experiencing stiffness in his limbs and nodules on his neck and hands, he was given a diagnosis of ankylosing spondylitis, a degenerative disease of the connective tissue. After suffering from a reaction to the drugs he had been given, he set out to take matters into his own hands to recover with the help of his doctor.

Norman checked himself into a hotel, took mega doses of intravenous injections of vitamin C, watched movies all day that made him laugh, and read humorous books. He intended to change his mental focus and vibration to one of good health. By watching comedies, he was focusing on happy thoughts. In time, he experienced an improvement with a withdrawal of symptoms and eventually regained most of his lost freedom of movement.

The God Within

Our thoughts are like prayers and create invisible energy that eventually turns into matter or our experiences. Since there is no judgment around this energy, it delivers based on our thoughts, and it is important to realize how creative our thoughts are. Know that prayers are always answered when asked, whether or not we believe that.

I was surprised to learn that Jesus never performed a healing on anyone unless they first asked. He saw the perfection in everyone and felt people were perfect even if they believed they were ill. I admire the strength of Jesus' belief of allowing everyone their own perspective. His type of thinking reduces fear and stress and enhances our relationships and connections with others. If you let go of judgment of others' choices, and accept them totally, joy will result for you and for the other person.

You are the force in everything. As you think so shall you be.

Christianity says – "The kingdom of heaven is within you."

In Islam – "Those who know themselves know their God."

Buddhism – "Look within, you are the Buddha."

Yoga – "God dwells within you as you."

Confucianism – "Heaven and Earth and Humans are of one body"

Ancient Hindus Text – "By understanding the self all is known."

The meaning of all these messages is that God is not so much to be found, but discovered within you.

Exercise 1:

Look back over your life and list the movies you have enjoyed the most. Did you pick movies that brought you laughter, or ones with strong moral messages? Did you choose a drama, a romantic story, or one with a historical theme? Then see how this movie represents a mirror of your life or your desires or your personality. The movie can give you great insight about yourself and your personal preferences and help you make important future decisions regarding career options, hidden desires, and relationship issues that may have been hidden within your subconscious mind.

Chapter Eleven
We Can Choose Again

The greatest discoveries a man makes, one of his great surprises, is to find he can do what he was afraid he couldn't do.

Henry Ford

After my brother's death at the age of fifty-eight, from 1995 to 1997 was a period of spiritual and self-growth, and the beginning of a new career direction using Feng Shui. Knowing that life consists of being truly in the moment, I started to realize a dream I had put off for fifteen years: the wish to open a design center for students and professional designers to team up together. I wanted the students to have an opportunity to work with clients while studying interior design. At the same time they would have a chance to assist and mentor with professional designers on various projects. I was looking forward to teaching students and I was excited that I could also include a study on Feng Shui.

I took one of my clients, a very creative businessman, who would soon be retiring, and his wife to dinner to propose my idea for the design center, in hopes he might consider investing with me. He had a large portfolio and could help fund my project. From personal experience, I knew he would enjoy supporting and inspiring young designers.

I took him by the building I wanted to lease, a building I had been previously retained to remodel, converting a bank into a real estate office. It was now vacant. My attempts to get the key or have a realtor meet me to show my client the building were met with a lot of resistance. It was as though I was not supposed to show him this building. Even though I had offered several appointment times, the leasing agent couldn't make it at a time that was convenient for my client. I left my investor with my proposal without his seeing the building. Since I had manifested an interested investor and found a building, I decided it would be wise to retain a lawyer to help me with the leasing agreement.

I was learning that manifesting was all about getting clear on what you want, knowing it will occur, and then being able to let go of the results of how and when, and letting the non-physical energy of the Universe take over to bring the idea into reality. I had been working on increasing prosperity in my life. To improve my financial situation, I chose to take a class at a church called 4T Prosperity. The teacher had told us, "When I was in law school I wanted a beautiful Victorian house."

After class, when I asked the instructor if he was working as a lawyer, he told me he specialized in negotiating leases for major corporations. I was surprised: just what I had asked for had occurred again. He agreed to consult with me, and I told him I would bring in my proposal and executive business plan. I also told him I had spent a lot of time and effort putting it together and trusted he would not lose it. When I came to class the following week, he informed me he had misplaced it. I confidently told him I knew he would find it. Then I got a hunch that I should read the building for the Feng Shui potential energy.

I took a compass reading on the building and discovered the building was not good for people or money. The remedies required to change this energy could not be done on this particular commercial space due to the location of the building. When I spoke with my lawyer friend, he suggested I look at industrial spaces with a commercial real estate broker. He felt an industrial space would be much more cost-effective than a retail space.

The real estate broker I consulted told me he had just returned from skiing in Heavenly Valley, and I felt I was being divinely guided. He informed me the building I had wanted to rent had been a bank in the seventies and had been "the only bank in the area that had gone bankrupt in 1978."

The building was vacant because my former remodeling client, the owner of the real estate company, had passed away and his wife could not keep up the expenses without him. Looking back, I can see why I couldn't get into the building in the first place, and why my lawyer friend had lost my business proposal. I was being divinely guided not to rent the space. Fortunately, I was learning to become more aware, and to watch for signs from the Universe. Thanks to my Feng Shui calculations, my intuition was confirmed!

Even though I had a business plan, an investor, and a leasing advisor, I still had no building. When we let go, our desires come to us in mysterious ways we could never predict. While shopping in the mall, I met a woman looking at a four-poster bed identical to the one I was selling. After studying Feng Shui, I had learned that four-poster beds are not the best for sleep. The posts do not promote sleep and can be mistaken for someone standing next to your bed if you should wake during the night. I approached her and said I was selling a bed just like it. She told me she was a hairdresser and her father was an interior designer, who would purchase the bed for her. We exchanged business cards.

I made an appointment to have her style my hair, and when I went to see her, I told her how I was planning to create a design center. "That's funny," she said, "my father has always wanted to do that. Here is his phone number, call him, and tell him I sent you to talk with him." Her father and I talked about the idea. He had a 10,000 square-foot warehouse with an upholstery factory in the back. His busy schedule held up the meeting with my investor, and when we all got together, they both wanted me to be a partner. After giving the arrangement a great deal of thought, I felt I wanted a short-term contract to set up the center but I didn't want to be a partner.

The hesitation of working with a partner could have been coming from my past-life experience of working with a partner who took the gold and left me to die. At that time I was unaware of the past-life experience and only knew I had an uneasy feeling about working with a partner.

Understandably, my friend, the investor, did not want to go in without me as a partner, and the interior designer expressed fear of carrying it alone. Since I didn't feel comfortable working with someone coming from a place of fear, I chose to pull out of the whole situation. I knew my goal to help students experience first-hand how to work professionally with a real client might manifest in another form.

Six months later I was hired to teach Feng Shui and Lighting, and oversee an Interior Design Presentation Lab at a local college, working with interior design students again. It had been five years since I had taught there. I feel my desire and thoughts about working with students manifested in the form of this teaching position. Sometimes we have to actually experience something to know if it is what we want.

* * *

Author and metaphysician Louise Hay's example of always being able to choose again had a great impact on me. In her book, she wrote that we can have anything we desire: we just have to ask, believe it is possible, and be patient for the perfect results. It's like going to dinner and ordering food from the menu, she says. We then sit and wait with a knowing that it will come as we ordered it. We don't follow the waiter into the kitchen to make sure the cook does it right; we trust it will be what we ordered. If it doesn't come to our liking, we can send it back to be prepared differently. That is very much how the universe brings us exactly what we ask for, if we are willing to let go of how something will come to us.

I have found that if we can get to the subconscious mind and reprogram it to support our desires, things often fall in place effortlessly. I decided to teach my business associates the importance of making a list of affirmations. I had them record their list on a cassette tape with relaxing music in the background, so they could listen to it at night before falling asleep.

Out of ten people, only two followed through and did the exercise. The results for those two people were one hundred percent successful. Each shared that in six weeks they had accomplished a goal they recorded on the tape. Each reported that every single night they listened to the cassette before retiring. They did not change anything else in their life. They discovered that in addition to achieving a successful business goal, they fell asleep faster and slept better, waking up more refreshed.

I have recorded several such tapes and have always seen improvements in my life from the affirmations lodging in my subconscious mind.

While visiting a friend in Maui, I decided to relax in their beautiful tropical garden and make a new recording. Since my friend's husband, who was working at a radio station, had a great voice, I asked and he agreed to read and record a list of my affirmations.

As I was preparing my list, I went to a local bookstore. While casually browsing through the metaphysical books, I read a passage in one that said, "If you are planning to make a tape recording of your affirmations, it is best to put it in your own voice." It is also said that your subconscious mind is more receptive to your own voice. Although I had asked my friend to record, I was still open to Universal guidance, and when it came, it inspired me to follow my original plan to record in my own voice. I learned once again to remain open and let go, following God's magical signs.

Many of us are asking on a very unconscious level. The Universe doesn't decide if it would be good for us, it just brings in what we ask for. Through that experience, it is up to us to decide if it is what we want, which explains why people often say experience is the best teacher. If the experience is not what we decide we want, then we can choose again—the true meaning of having free choice.

Perspective is King

The Universe never judges our choices. That fact is illustrated clearly in this old Taoist story about a man whose horse ran away. When it happened, all his neighbors came over and said, "Gee, it's really awful your horse ran away and so forth..." The man replied, "Maybe, maybe not." The next day the horse came back and brought twenty really nice wild horses with it. All the neighbors observed how great it was this man now had all these horses – and the man said, "Maybe, maybe not." The next day the man's son was out tying to break one of the horses, got thrown off and broke his leg. All the neighbors talked about how awful that was and so forth, and the man said, "Maybe, maybe not." The next day the army came by conscripting young men to fight in some war, but they didn't take the man's son because he had a broken leg. It is clear that man is the one who judges and causes his reality from his judgment of circumstances. "Perspective is King."

This story illustrates why experiences are not specifically good or bad. With our limited perspectives, we may not be able to see the bigger picture. What could have happened if we had made a different choice or if we had not been late for an appointment? Allowing *what is* to just be is to be more allowing and accepting everything to be in perfect order. It is a way to go with the flow, and reduce stress. Studies have show that the reduction of stress contributes to our good health.

A recent client of mine, Ramesh, told me his wife Suzanne's grandmother had recently passed. He said his wife, who missed her grandmother, would often sit and speak to her grandmother, wanting to continue her close relationship even though she could no longer see her. One day while driving, Suzanne stopped at a red light. When the light turned green, Suzanne's arms were frozen at the steering wheel; she was unable to move the car forward. She was astonished to find that her hands were literally stuck to the steering wheel. A few seconds later, a speeding truck crossed in front of her; it had run through the red light. Suzanne told Ramesh she felt it was an intervention by her grandmother, who was watching over her. To me, it was an example of divine intervention.

Ramesh said he feels that what we often perceive to be good or bad is really the perfect timing of the Universe. When we are bothered that we are running late, Ramesh suggested, "What if the reason for the delay was to keep us out of harm's way by avoiding an accident or an unwanted experience?" I could not help but agree with him. After the terrorists' attack of the New York twin towers in 2001, there were numerous reports of people being late for work, unexpected events that caused delays, illnesses that kept people home, and endless stories that made so many thankful for the interruption of their normal morning routine on that day. By letting go and trusting that there is never an accident, we are able to be more allowing and accepting.

As our thinking continues to realize the unlimited possibilities we have in every situation, it is important to put forth a clear intention by going within and realizing how we are feeling. Our feelings are the thermostat for our living. With each experience we encounter, our feelings help us to get clear so we can continue to ask for what we desire. Honoring our feelings is to give respect to who we are as individuals. Fear is the basis for our lack of love, wealth, friendships, good health and pleasure.

People operating from constant fear are those who may never want to choose based on the fear that by making a poor decision, they will be judged, ridiculed, criticized or ultimately face embarrassment. They may feel they will never get another chance to choose again, which causes them paralysis in moving forward to try anything. Or they may feel that they may be seen as foolish. Society expects us to be the same, and if we conform to another's expectations over our own desires, we have lost a part of our soul. When you are able to identify the fear, you will be able to move through it with awareness and let go of what has held you from your true essence. The best way to get on the other side of fear is to move through it.

As we hesitate to move in the direction of our passion, the Universe may give us an experience to help us become more aware. Sometimes those experiences come with heartache. If we choose not to acknowledge and wake up, we may get another experience that gets our attention in a bigger way. Know that change does not have to come with pain because we always have choices. Our biggest choice is how we respond to every experience. Coming from a place of love softens the pain, and helps to eliminate fear, since we cannot feel more than one emotion at a time. Love heals.

Love yourself and others and allow yourself and others to experience for themselves who they really are. Know that you can always choose again.

Exercise 1:

This exercise requires a tape recorder. Using the positive affirmations suggested in the back of the book or those you have made up, you will tape affirmations so that you can listen to them when going to sleep at night or during the day while driving, exercising, or doing housework. I have found it is very important how your affirmations are worded. It is also important to add an emotional verb before your affirmation such as: *I am excited to receive a steady flow of income that allows me to live my dreams.* Be sure to put your affirmations in the present tense. By beginning your affirmation with "I am," you reinforce your desire and confidence.

The affirmations are done to raise your vibration and place a positive thought in your subconscious mind. When you add an emotional verb to your affirmation, it helps create excitement and energy around your desires. Once you have your list of affirmations written out, then tape record them in your own voice with soft music in the background.

Music also has vibration: positive and not so positive. It has been said that classical music has a very high positive vibration. That could be why surgeons often listen to classical music while doing surgery. Be sure the music you select helps you relax because you will be listening to it as you fall asleep. You will find this recording will also allow you to go to sleep easily and have a much deeper sleep. By listening to positive affirmations in your own voice, you replace any anxiety in your mind that may hinder your progress.

If you find affirmations boring and too repetitious for you, be more creative by describing the way your life will be when you have accomplished your present goals and desires. Walk through your entire day as if your dreams have already occurred, giving as great deal of detail and emotion into describing the life you want to live. It's almost like writing a novel or a script with you being the main character. Be sure to listen to the tape every night as you fall asleep. The recording is best if it is 20 to 30 minutes in length. If you fall asleep while listening that is fine, because the affirmations and positive desires will go into your subconscious even if you are asleep. See the affirmations section at the back of this book for instructions for daytime or nighttime recording.

Chapter Twelve
Synchronicities and Messages from our Environments

Before we can make friends with anyone else, we must first make friends with ourselves.

First Lady, Eleanor Roosevelt

As I continue to release old thoughts and old ideas I see that everything, everyone, and all situations are a mirror for my thoughts. So much information is constantly being revealed to me to help me see who I am in each new moment. We are expanding beings, creative and constantly flowing with new ideas. Our thoughts help us choose new experiences, and our emotions help us decide what feels best.

Are you in touch with your emotions? Your inner emotions are the best guidance you have. Six months before my father passed I felt deep sadness. It was as if I knew on a deeper subconscious level that he would soon be choosing to make his transition. I say choosing because I believe we each choose everything we experience in life. Our thoughts vibrate and attract to us people and situations that are like-minded.

The following is an example of how the Universe gives us information. If, for instance, you are always being criticized by one person in particular, it's an indication you feel the need to be criticized by that person. If you look deeply within yourself, you may be able to find reasons why you feel the person delivering the criticism is revealing your hidden feelings. You may have deep hidden guilt concerning that person, especially if they are the only person from whom you are receiving the criticism. These hidden feelings of guilt may be attracting the criticism to you.

Wake Up to Your Intuition

Look at every situation as a gift and you will be able to accept experiences in the moment with gratitude. The information is for the purpose of helping you heal. Once you realize you are the one doing the self-criticism and that's why you've had the experience, you can do what you need to do to let go of the guilt and heal. Sometimes, you may need to ask for forgiveness from the person. Sometimes, it's just a matter of being more aware and realizing you do not need to experience self-criticism. In that case, you can let go. When you let go of your need to be criticized, the critic may magically stop their critical comments when you are together. At least it seems like magic to me. We are truly responsible for our own lives and our own feelings and experiences.

One evening at a restaurant with my husband I had a revealing experience. I had been working earlier that day on shifting some of my limiting beliefs. Once we are aware of a limiting belief, we can make a decision to release that belief, and shift our thinking to something positive and self-loving or to continue to hold onto the old belief. It is always our choice, but once the awareness is there, then the shifting becomes quite simple. I had excused myself to go to the restroom, and as I walked past a woman waiting in the reception area, I noticed she was talking on the phone and heard her say as I was passing: "Well, it is actually getting better for me now." It echoed my thoughts since I was also getting better as I released my limiting beliefs.

On another occasion, I was at my dentist's office concentrating on being relaxed before the dentist began. I heard music from a local radio station as he began working on me. I'll always remember how comforted I felt when I heard this song playing on the radio: "He's Got the Whole World in his Hands." I knew it was no accident that in that moment I received the supportive message through the radio helping me to be more relaxed.

One night while walking my dog, as it was getting dark, I said to myself, "I am very safe here walking with my dog." During that walk I saw at least three police cars pass by me and knew my vibration of being safe was true. Our environment is always a reflection of our thoughts. Learning to read your environment takes practice but it's very supportive and beneficial to validate your feelings and beliefs and get your personal truth.

Often, I hear people say, "I had a hunch, or feeling right before something problematic happened." They will say they ignored their intuition, but clearly remember having a thought to change directions, go a different way, or just make a different choice. When the hunch has been ignored, they have said they regret not listening to that non-physical nudge from the

Universe. Some have called this divine guidance, others refer to Angelic intervention.

When a person starts to wake up to their own intuition and feelings, the synchronicities begin to appear all around them. I found that it felt almost overwhelming because I was getting messages from everywhere validating for me that I was making the right choice or that I was in the right place. I had a past life regression and came home one evening and the show I was watching on TV had an identical story line of the regression I had experienced that day. I felt it was validating the hypnosis session and also indicating to me that I was still processing the information and that the thoughts were still active in my vibration.

Even the little things tell us we are connected to a more infinite power. Whenever I glance at the clock upon awakening or during the day, I constantly see how the numbers are lined up with 8:08, 9:39, 10:01 or 11:11.

I also see how license plates often bring us positive messages if we pay attention. I have come to understand for me that the numbers 333 means the higher masters are bringing me a message, so pay attention. On my walk one day as my husband and I strolled down a beautiful pine tree-lined street near our home, a hawk flew towards us and landed on a branch in a nearby tree, and remained there about three feet above our heads as we walked under the branch of the tree. On another occasion my husband was leaving our home to run an errand and he turned to look back at our home and saw a large hawk sitting on the chimney of our house. He snapped a photo of it to show me with his cell phone. It was so large I thought at first it was a person standing on the chimney.

Awareness is the Key to Letting Go

Awareness is the key to letting go, especially if you are challenged by procrastination. The awareness helps us identify our passions in order to follow our hearts. When we are more aware of our beliefs about life experiences, relationships, and our environment, we can always understand ourselves better and choose to shift the thoughts that no longer serve us. We can become our own best friend. No longer do we need to get validation or the opinions of others. The world around you is your best indicator of what direction you need to go to enjoy a more fulfilling life, because it is a reflection of your inner being.

Learning to interpret your environment and surroundings is a personal thing. Often things mean something different to you than they do to others. It is important that you trust your thoughts. When you wake up from a night of sleep, your dreams can give you great insight as well. Many people keep a note pad next to their bed so they can write down their dreams and use them to understand their feelings and life choices. This practice helps you to always choose the things that bring you passion, to let go of choices that do not feel good to you, or will not take you into your passion.

When we are truly aligned with God's energy, we are in perfect health. If we are having health challenges, it is important to look at your thoughts and beliefs to determine how you may have separated yourself from the belief that Source creates perfect health. As Deepak Chopra teaches us, we each have the ingredients within us to heal ourselves. I believe perfect health starts with our thoughts. When we believe we can have perfect health, solutions appear. If we desire perfect health and focus on our perfection, we attract to us the solutions to help us have that perfect health.

If we have a hidden belief that we need to be punished or need to experience pain, we will attract the pain and suffering we feel we deserve. This could be from a belief acquired in childhood, and is often a belief from a thought carried over from a previous life. If you desire something new, yet you keep doing the same thing over and over and get the same results, wake up to the messages all around you bringing you signals of support. If you are thinking of making a change, ask for guidance, and then watch how the Universe answers. If the answer is not clearly evident, ask for the answer to be revealed to you with greater clarity.

Exercise 1:

The Universe, what some refer to as angels, your magical inner self, or what others call God is that magical energy that helps to manifest your world. If we acknowledge and recognize the magic that comes to us each day, we will begin to attract more to us. Some have suggested keeping a gratitude journal and that would work well for this exercise. The more grateful you become and the more you acknowledge your gratitude, the more things come to you to be grateful for.

Start a journal of magical occurrences. A magical occurrence is a synchronicity that happens when you feel you are in the right place at the right time and everything just seems to go smoothly for you.

This exercise will help you to not only identify the magic around you that is occurring all the time; it will increase your awareness, your intuition and help you to understand how to tap into the magic all the time. This exercise helps you form habits that will help your life flow effortlessly, and it will help you trust and let go of the old habits of having to work hard to make something happen.

Think a positive thought and let go. You may want to record the successes that have occurred from your "God can" requests from Chapter Two. Give your request time and watch what occurs. Then be sure to add the experience to your journal. Your writings will help increase your belief of possibilities, allowing you to expand your creations, and will help you reinforce that you are being supported by an infinite power, far greater than anything we could imagine or describe in words.

If you keep this notebook near your bed, you can record these occurrences at the end of your day. You can also use the book to keep track of any dreams you may have had, and to list those things you are grateful for. Write down your dreams immediately upon awakening, whether it's in the middle of the night or in the morning, it is important to jot down as much as you can remember about the specific dream. Our dreams bring us wisdom and insight, increasing our awareness, and help us to release stress and challenges we may encounter in our everyday lives.

Chapter Thirteen
The Law of Attraction

Law of attraction attracts to you everything you need, according to the nature of your thought. Your environment and financial condition are the perfect reflection of your habitual thinking. Thoughts rule the world.

Dr. Joseph Edward Murphy, Surgeon

The law of attraction has been demonstrated to me over and over again. There is no doubt in my mind that everything we do and have in our lives originates from our thoughts. By the law of attraction, we have been given the greatest gift of all: the gift of free choice and free will. The more powerful your emotion is about something, the faster you create the related experience. It's that simple.

Do you wonder why you haven't created what you want? Perhaps there's conflict between what you say you want, and what you truly desire. Lack of clarity and emotion will delay your experience. Holding onto the control of how and when you will receive your dream is a big factor as well. Letting go is the secret that creates the magic. Not being aware of the importance of letting go keeps us wondering why others are able to move forward while we stay stuck.

The Law of Attraction awakened me to the reasons behind my personal experiences from 1997 to 1998. When I attended a seminar during that period, participants were directed to make a vision board, a poster with pictures of things we would like to have in our lives. We were told that if we took our vision boards home and placed them where we could look at them daily, the reality of the images we placed on the poster would appear magically in our lives.

I thought seriously about what I wanted in my life. I remember finding travel brochures in the lobby of the hotel where I was staying and cutting out the words England, France and Belgium to place on the poster board. I'd never thought about going to Belgium before I added it to my board but did it anyway, along with a picture of a new silver Toyota 4 Runner. As a dog lover, I cut out a picture of a German shepherd; I had been dreaming of such a dog, but one over a year old and housebroken. At that time we were between houses and living in a townhouse, where I could not have pets.

Nine months later, in the spring of 1998, I was speaking to a travel agent to plan a trip to Greece for my birthday. When I hung up the phone, I thought to myself, "This trip is more than we want to spend right now; I know another destination will appear." Within a day, my friend DeAnna phoned and asked me if I would like to go to Belgium and stay at their timeshare condo. She had arranged for it and was unable to use it. When I looked at my vision board with Belgium on it, I began to see how the law of attraction works.

Most important, once I'd put the names of the countries on the board, I did not think about how the trip would materialize. I couldn't have imagined the way it developed in such perfect timing. Not only did we go to Belgium but we were able to take the underwater Chunnel to England, and on another day the train to France. We visited all three countries in the same trip.

Before we left, I learned how our words strongly create our experiences. When I visited my mom before leaving, she told me, "I will picture you touring all the museums." Because I wanted to plan my own trip and have a more spontaneous time, I replied, "Don't picture me in museums, I've spent too many years in art history classes and studying art. I just want to have a spontaneous and fun trip."

A few days after arriving in Belgium, we took a one-day trip to France by train on a Tuesday. We had a great time touring Paris, but when we got to the Louvre Museum, we discovered Tuesday was the only day the Louvre was closed. I knew right away what I had said about not wanting to be inside museums had manifested according to the law of attraction!

I learned I quickly had to "let go" of my disappointment and turn my attention to all the other wonderful new experiences I was having. I couldn't change the hours of the Louvre that day, but I could change my attitude from disappointment to pleasure, and to continue to anticipate and enjoy what was to come. The faster we let go, the quicker we can move on to joy and pleasurable experiences. Now I have a good reason to return to Paris, and I will be sure to put forth an intention that I would love to tour the Louvre. Due to my strong emotions about going back, and according to the law of attraction, I am confident I will have that opportunity.

Let Go and Celebrate

I saw this same ability to "let go" quickly happen with my daughter-in-law. My husband and I, our son, Chris, his wife, Erin, and their two-year-old son, Tanner, took my mother to Disneyland to celebrate her 90th birthday. We took turns going on the rides since Tanner was too young for many of them. In between rides one of us would be walking Tanner in the stroller. At one point the stroller was unattended, and when Erin returned from a ride, she was disappointed to see her expensive sunglasses were missing from the stroller handles. Although we retraced our steps and looked everywhere, even the lost and found, we had no luck finding them.

I was impressed and pleased to see how quickly Erin was able to let go of her disappointment. Instead of feeling miserable and affecting us with her loss, like many would do to attract attention and sympathy, she quickly let go of her disappointment and enjoyed the rest of the day with us.

The law of attraction works all of the time, every time, whether or not you believe it. When I first noticed things manifesting from my words, I noticed that what I desired would take about nine months to appear. Since I was previously unaware of the influence my thoughts, words and emotions had on my life, I didn't know how fast other desires had manifested in the past. Currently, my thoughts manifest my desires in weeks, days and sometimes within hours.

In 2001, I purchased a new silver Toyota 4 Runner, an exact match of the picture on my vision board. We also purchased a home that year. I was beginning to learn how the magic of the law of attraction was working. At the beginning of summer, I began saying lightheartedly that everything I touched turned to gold. Lo and behold, we purchased a house on Calle de Oro, which means street of gold in Spanish.

The purchase of our home came with much letting go. I had been looking for a home for over a year. Because of what I learned about Feng Shui, there were lots of requirements for the home I desired. Sal would drive me to various newly listed homes, and I would take a compass reading to see if they were suitable. I failed to realize that all I needed to do was to get clear about what I wanted to feel in my new home and to just let go.

We found a home that did not exactly match my desired compass reading, but there were many other things we liked about the home, and we began negotiations. The negotiations lasted almost two months with no resolution. "It must not be the right time to purchase a home," I said to myself and I let go. When a realtor phoned about a home she felt I might like, I had let go so well that I told her, "No, I'm done looking." Fortunately, a friend encouraged me to reconsider, and so I did.

On my first visit to the home, I noticed the same oval stained-glass white front door as the house I had been negotiating for over the last few months. The front door had been one of my favorite things about the other home. I also remember I had stood on the balcony of my townhouse looking out over the great view and saying to myself, "This is the type of view I would like from my next home." Even though this new home was in a different city, the view was almost identical. I had also asked for a view of the ocean and, sure enough, we do have a small view of the ocean from our backyard. The last undeniable factor of how well letting go really works was that the compass reading was the exact same reading I had been looking for over the past year.

The third desire on the vision board was my German Shepherd. Once into my new home, I knew I could now have the dog I had longed for since the loss of our dog in 1995. When we moved in November 2001, I realized I must let go and patiently wait for an inspiration to act and for my wish to come true. On Saturday, December 17 at 4:30 P.M., I got my inspiration and told my husband we needed to go to the pound and look at the dogs. I don't know why I got the inspiration that day. Maybe I was just tired of waiting, but I do know I got an undeniable hunch I needed to go that day. "It's late, and they close at 5:00 P.M.," Sal pointed out, but I insisted and so we went.

When we arrived at the dog pound, we were presented with a year-old German shepherd that had been brought in earlier that day. Just as I had asked, she matched the picture on my vision board. We both knew she was just the dog for us after the loss of our previous German shepherd in 1995 to hip problems. Now eight years old, my dog has been a true companion. I loved the fact that she was housebroken, just as I had asked. We learned the previous owner, who had owned her since she was a puppy, had brought her in because his other dogs did not get along with her. It was as if he had been keeping her for me until she reached a year old, just as I requested. She was a pure breed, more than I had asked for, and the owner gave us her papers, which showed she was born Aug. 17, 2000. I am always amazed at how our words, thoughts, and desires manifest our reality.

Do our Beliefs Follow us After Death?

From my experiences that have impacted me over the years, I have concluded that belief has everything to do with what we experience in our lives and possibly what we experience after the physical death of our bodies. People who feel they will meet Jesus after death will most likely meet him. It seems to me that what we believe is what occurs in our lives. Wayne Dyer has always taught, "Believe it and you will see it." He does not say, "Wait to see it and then you can believe it.

Why wouldn't our beliefs continue on in the energy of our thoughts after the release of our physical body, continuing to create our experiences in the non-physical world? Those who have a strong belief in Jesus here on earth, they would tend to be more likely to be greeted in the afterlife by Jesus, whereas those who belief in Buddha or other religious leaders might attract their more familiar figures after their death.

Allowing each of us to have our opinions, choices, and preferences, letting go of judgment and comparing ourselves to others attracts love and the magic of life. Placing expectations on others is the basis for feelings of betrayal. We set ourselves up to expect certain actions from others and when they do not follow through with our vision, we feel betrayed. If we could let go of all the expectations we project upon others, it allows each of us to be in the flow and allows the Universe to deliver its magic.

To create the life we desire, we must become aware of what we believe. Uncovering what is deep in our subconscious is very important in fulfilling our dreams. As I've mentioned, according to the law of attraction, what you think becomes what you experience. Why do many people complain that the law of attraction has not worked for them? Most likely it is because they are unaware of the limiting beliefs hidden deep within the subconscious. Once aware of these subconscious beliefs, we can decide to let go of those that keep us from living our greatest potential.

The law of attraction is working in your life. If you are uncomfortable with believing you may have lived a past life, find another method to help you realize and uncover your deep beliefs. Focus on the method that feels good to you, replacing thoughts that no longer serve your present goals. We all change and grow. Change is constant and is the only thing we can count on.

Being able to let go and allow change to occur brings confidence, support, and success. When one door closes, another door opens. Let us not fear the loss, but welcome the new. Whatever gives you a feeling of satisfaction needs to be included in your thoughts and experiences. If letting go is challenging for you, then you may need to experience lots of different methods until you find what works best to help you let go.

Exercise 1:

Making a vision board, always a pleasure to do as a group exercise, will be a fun creative project. Studies have shown that pictures viewed regularly go deep into the subconscious mind and help attract what you desire into your life. Cut pictures and positive words out of a magazine and paste them on a poster board. Put all the things you desire on the board to make a beautiful collage. You can add actual pictures of family and friends. If you want to get slimmer, cut out a picture of a slim body and glue a picture of your face on it.

Be sure to include pictures that illustrate perfect health and vitality, fun activities and hobbies, places you might like to travel, the amount of income you would enjoy having in your bank account, words indicating financial freedom, or being a multi-millionaire. Include the type of home you would love to live in and the car you would enjoy driving. You may even want to visit your local dealership and be photographed sitting in your dream car.

Remember to list charities that you would like to support and any other things you desire to attract into your life. When you finish your vision board, have it reduced and photo copied in color to carry in your date book, post at your office, or have with you at all times in your briefcase. I have my vision board in my office above my computer so I can view it easily all the time.

It is good to make a new vision board regularly. If you have children, encourage them to make their own vision boards.

Chapter Fourteen
Letting Go to Change the World

What lies before us and what lies behind us are small matters compared to what lies within us. And when we bring what is within out into the world, miracles happen.

Henry David Thoreau, Author

Letting go is a major issue in all our lives. If we can become more allowing and let go with ease of: blame, resentment, anger, sadness, clutter (possessions that take up too much room or possessions attached to unwanted emotions like grief, sadness or anger), our lives would be filled with joy. Wouldn't it be wonderful to let go of unwanted habits, thoughts, and even the extra weight we carry in our bodies, which symbolizes the weight of the worries we carry from our association with the physical world? I have discussed many of these topics in previous chapters.

One of the prominent issues I hear about a great deal is blaming others for what has clearly been our own choice in life. How can someone blame another for their experiences in life when we each have free will and free choice? Just because we make a choice we don't want doesn't mean we don't have a choice. Our greatest knowledge and wisdom comes from making choices we did not like. Looking back years later and blaming another for your disappointment defeats the wisdom gained from the experience and keeps us from owning our power. Those who welcome their poor choices live life to the fullest and become stronger in the process.

Many people blame someone else for their misfortune, whether it's a partner in business, a spouse, another driver in an accident, a neighbor, a boss, a friend or a relative. The person who blames never factors in the original action that began with their choice to be in the location of the event or relationship. Those who have problems with relationships have had choices everyday, but have chosen not to listen to the voice inside advising them that the relationship is not working. Years pass and those affected look back with regret and blame.

Learning to let go takes practice, like anything else we want to accomplish. When there is fear associated with the action, it becomes more challenging. Fear begins to diminish with repetition and practice. If it does not diminish, there is a hidden belief that needs to be revealed so it can be cleared. If you have gotten to this chapter and haven't taken the time to do one of the exercises in this book, you are avoiding discovering what might be keeping you from having the magical life you desire.

How do we practice letting go? We can start by attentive listening in a conversation with someone we care about. Wait until the person has finished speaking, count to ten and then repeat back to them what they have just said. By doing this you are letting go of what you're thinking about and giving the other person one hundred percent of your attention. Isn't that what we want when we share with others? We want to be heard and acknowledged. We want the other person to let go of their agenda. Letting go with no attachment to the result in conversations brings about stronger relationships with your spouse, children, friends, and family, and also increases business when working in the field of sales.

When I finally realized how much simpler life would be if I could let go easily, have less stuff and better relationships, I started focusing on my words and actions in conversations. Then I went through my environment and took a close look at my home, gaining more knowledge about my thinking processes and what I was attracting. Consequently, I was able to make some positive choices that would help our whole family.

Due to financial challenges, in the late 1990s during a slow real estate market following the Desert Storm War, we decided to sell our home, and my journey of "letting go" continued. Since my husband had worked hard most of his life to provide his family with a very special place to live, he found the move difficult because our home was a reflection of his years of hard work. Once we decided to sell, it took another year-and-a-half to find a buyer for our 3400 square foot custom home on an acre of land. During that time I was forced to learn how to appreciate and enjoy the moment! What a gift that truly was, and it was only recently that I realized what I had learned.

Once we sold the house I had three months to pack to move. The new owner had the entire house painted outside before we moved, and I celebrated my birthday with a great party. During the last few days in the house, the dishwasher stopped working and the furnace would not go on. When I was on the phone with a friend, I noticed that the painter had unplugged my fountain, the outdoor Feng Shui remedy for prosperity. I stopped my conversation, went out to plug it in, and got back on the phone. Within minutes the furnace started up! I constantly saw examples of how the non-physical energy all around us was influenced by movement of energy in our environment.

We spent two full days packing. My oldest son packed up his room and moved his things a day early to our condo. On moving day he and his girlfriend joined my husband and me in packing. Our youngest son helped move all the large furniture and packed boxes into the rental truck. By 2 A.M. the house was empty, and we were ready to leave, but the truck had a dead battery and wouldn't start. Thanks to my youngest son's mechanic's skills, he got the truck running again, but the truck got stuck between the driveway and the street at the bottom of our steep driveway. My oldest son used his four-wheel drive truck to tow it from the wedged position. We now joke about how the house was filled with the Feng Shui energy of delays, attempting to hold on to us right up to the day we moved. I think I also had a resistance to letting go and things seemed to move forward ever so slowly.

At 5 A.M. we had all arrived at our new condo. To my surprise, my husband said, "Bye, I have to get to work." My older son slept in his new room. My youngest went to stay with friends, and I went to sleep at my parents' home. At one o'clock the next afternoon I came home and found my older son and three friends moving everything into our condo from the rental truck. He taught me an unforgettable lesson: take care of yourself so that when others really need you, you will be strong enough to help them. He has also taught me the importance of getting clear about my feelings, to take care of myself in order to get my needs met. Once I had completely let go, it seemed that everything began to move forward again with ease.

I have since learned that the best way to build strong relationships is by sharing one's feelings. Start with being honest with yourself, and speak your truth. No one can ever argue with your feelings. Feelings cannot be debated; they are not wrong, they are your truth. It is like desiring chocolate ice cream instead of vanilla. One choice does not make the other choice wrong, just different. Speaking your truth and sharing your feelings takes courage. Allowing others their truth without debate also takes courage. This is how we can heal the world. It is how we begin to open up to others, connecting on a level of feelings, universal to us all.

Love and Fear

I realized love and fear are like Yin and Yang, both important to maintain balance in our lives. One is not good and the other bad. Both are important to life, and when balanced help us to achieve a healthy lifestyle. Love connects us to each other, and fear protects us from going beyond our natural abilities. Is fear appropriate? Of course it is when we see the truth. Unfortunately, fear can be "fantasizing events appearing to be real." As long as we understand who we are and speak the truth, we can see that fear can be overcome. One of the best ways to overcome fear is through love.

Love is Being Able to Let Go

Love brings about change to help us all move forward to create a better world. "What is love?" I asked myself. I went on a long search to discover what love actually is. I discovered love has to come from within. You can't truly give love until you have genuinely experienced loving yourself. Love is being able to allow another to express his/her feelings without criticism, argument, or judging. Love allows each of us to have our own opinion, our own experience, to give without any attachment to the result, to have free choice in every moment. Love allows people to find their own answers. Love is Trust. *Love is being able to Let Go.* When we feel like we are not being respected, it is because we do not respect ourselves. Respect does not come from another; it comes from within. What we are feeling and thinking about ourselves is what we hear from others being reflected back to us. What we tell others, if we listen to ourselves closely, is what we need to hear.

Those who are in their joy are also in their passion. Passion is a state of love. It is impossible to be in fear when you are in love. The two cannot reside in the same moment. When we are in fear we create and attract to us exactly what we are resisting. Fear and love are vibrations of energy that attract to us what we focus on

The person who watches the news and becomes fearful, believing that something similar could happen to him or her, is the person most likely to create the same event in his/her own life. Pay attention the next time you hear about a child's abduction. Within a week of the news report, you may see two or three other reports of child abductions. When a person hears a report of something they strongly fear or identify with, the fear within them may attract the same experience, depending on how great their fear.

We are creative people; we all have the ability to create our own lives. Our minds are like computers, and we do not really know yet all the things the mind can do. What we don't know, and are unaware that we don't know, keeps us from moving forward to create the world we say we want, a world of peace. Opening our minds up to new ways of thinking allows us to release our fears.

Does Evil Exist?

Does evil exist? The university professor challenged his students with this question. "Did God create everything that exists?" A student bravely replied, "Yes, He did! Yes, sir." The professor answered, "If God created everything, then God created evil since evil exists, and according to the principal that our works define who we are, then God is evil." The professor was quite pleased with himself and boasted to the students that he had proven once more that the Christian faith was a myth.

Another student raised his hand and said, "Can I ask you a question, Professor?" "Of course," replied the professor. The student stood up and asked, "Professor, does cold exist?" The students snickered at the young man's question. The young man added, "In fact, sir, cold does not exist. According to the laws of physics, what we consider cold is in reality the absence of heat. Every body or object is susceptible to study when it has or transmits energy, and heat is what makes a body or matter have or transmit energy. Absolute zero (-460 degrees F) is the total absence of heat. Cold does not exist. We have created this word to describe how we feel if we do not have heat."

The student continued, "Professor, does darkness exist?" The professor responded, "Of course it does." The student said, "Once again, you are wrong, sir. Darkness does not exist either. Darkness is in reality the absence of light. Light we can study, but not darkness. A simple ray of light can break into a world of darkness and illuminate it. How can you know how dark a certain space is? You measure the amount of light present. Isn't this correct? Darkness is a term used by man to describe what happens when there is no light present."

Finally the young man asked the professor, "Sir, does evil exist?" Now uncertain, the professor responded, "Of course, as I have already said, we see it every day. It is in the daily example of man's inhumanity to man. It is in the multitude of crime and violence everywhere in the world. These manifestations are nothing else but evil."

To this the student replied, "Evil does not exist, sir, or at least it does not exist unto itself. Evil is simply the absence of God. It is just like darkness and cold, a word that man has created to describe the absence of God, God did not create evil. Evil is the result of what happens when man does not have God's love present in his heart. It's like the cold that comes when there is no heat or the darkness that comes when there is not light." The professor sat down. The young man's name was Albert Einstein.

Our feelings about our everyday life are critical to creating our dreams. Having to "be right" for some people can be more important than having life go smoothly and accomplishing their heart's desire. Some people cannot surrender to the idea that someone else may be right because they think it might cause them to be wrong. What if I told you there were no *right* or *wrong* thoughts, that everyone comes from their own perspective, unique to them, and each person has the right to think and believe the way they want? Based on our own thoughts, we attract to us different experiences that illustrate our desires, fears, dreams, likes and dislikes.

As a child, it is our nature to want to feel joy and happiness, and as children we understand how to create it for ourselves. No one ever has to decide for a child what to do to have fun. They explore and end up creating their own games. When we watch a young child explore, we may see them tearing apart a roll of toilet paper, playing in the cabinets with the pots and pans, or lying outside in the grass finding pictures in the clouds. What children do naturally when they are young is who they are.

The child who loves academics and is a high achiever in school does that out of passion. Another child may love music; another may love to give oral reports in front of the class. Every child has a passion, and the wise teacher and parent is the one who is able to see through the child's eyes! Making a reluctant student love to study and take tests is as difficult as making a person who is fearful of heights stand on the edge of a cliff. When the desire comes from within, magic happens!

My father wanted so much to bring happiness to other people that he attempted to do everything he could for others, often going far beyond what others expected of him. Through his actions I learned we can't make other people happy, they must figure that out for themselves when they go within to discover for themselves who they are. Life is like an Easter Egg Hunt: it's no fun when someone tells you where the eggs are hidden!

In the book *The Power of Now* by Eckhart Tolle, he stated, "This is no mere theory - the 1982 Aspect Experiment in France demonstrated that two once-connected quantum particles separated by vast distances remained somehow connected. If one particle was changed, the other changed - instantly. Scientists don't know the mechanics of how this faster-than-the-speed-of-light travel can happen, though some theorists suggest that this connection takes place via doorways into higher dimensions."

What inspired me with this statement was that if one-half of the particle changes, the other half changes automatically without ever doing a thing. This fact helped me realize that by focusing on and improving myself, I will automatically impact and improve the lives of my children and grandchildren. Change works like a set of dominos, as one domino falls, it sets off a chain reaction affecting all the other dominos in the path of the first to fall.

The wonderful verse below was one my father gave me during a time I was struggling to accept something I wanted to change. It came from the Omaha Home for Boys. I hope it will help you in your search to enjoy life, giving you permission to let go of changing others and instead appreciate yourself and discover who you are!

*

Changing the World

*

When I was a young man, I wanted to change the world.

I found it was difficult to change the world, so I tried to change my nation.

When I found I couldn't change the nation, I began to focus on my town.

I couldn't change my town. And as an older man I tried to change my family.

Now, as an old man, I realize the only thing I can change is myself,

And suddenly I realize that if long ago I had changed myself,

I could have made an impact on my family.

My family and I could have made an impact on our town.

Their impact could have changed the nation and...
I could, indeed, have changed the world.

Exercise 1:

Make a list of all the ways you treat yourself. Think of things you choose to do that give you support. Do you find your list is lean? If so, begin to make a list of all the ways you can treat yourself. It could be that your list includes taking thirty minutes every day to exercise. Maybe taking a swim in a pool, or taking a walk in nature, getting a soothing massage, or just relaxing in a spa. For some it might be to set aside time for a relaxing bath, or to purchase something you never purchase for yourself, like a special piece of jewelry, cologne or perfume. Do anything that makes you feel supported. It could be to let go of cleaning your home once a week and hire a cleaning crew to help you. It is important to continue to give yourself love doing something every day consistently that brings you joy and causes you to feel good abut yourself.

Affirmations

These affirmations listed below are to be used for the exercise at the end of Chapter Four. Be sure if you are using these affirmations while going to sleep at night that you begin your tape recording with a relaxation of your body as listed below. Conclude the affirmations with a positive affirmation for wakening refreshed and calm after a good night's sleep. This will put the intention into your mind as you begin to fall sleep. Other affirmations can be recorded for daytime listening if you prefer. I prefer listening when going to sleep and have found the results come within six weeks or less. I encourage you to take the time to make your own recording. When writing your own personal affirmations, be sure to start the affirmation in the wording that it is already in your life: "I am." Pick and choose from the affirmations listed below those that fit for your life or write your own. Keep your affirmations to six main subjects or less for ease in manifesting.

Use these affirmations to relax your body in order to sleep deeply:

I am feeling very relaxed.

My feet are feeling very relaxed.

The energy in my legs flows freely up from my feet.

As I listen to the music I drift into a deeper sleep.

My hips are relaxed as they sink deeply into the surface where I am. I am moving forward making positive choices to support and nurture myself.

I love myself. I am free.

The energy continues to flow through my whole body as I relax. I trust the process of life. All I need is always taken care of. I am safe.

I have lots of support. People show up in my life at just the right time to assist me so that I move forward easily and effortlessly.

My upper body and arms are flowing with healing energy. I am free to move forward. My heart is filled with love moving forward with ease.

My neck & shoulders are so relaxed. I feel all my muscles relax.

My face is comfortable, I am feeling light, my mouth, nose, and ears are becoming light as I let go and allow relaxation to drift across my face and entire head.

My eyes are healthy and my vision gets better and better each day. I see clearly the open way. I accelerate on my path. I see clearly the perfect plan for my life.

I am clear about my purpose and how to live my purpose with balance in my life.

Only positive, loving, and supportive thoughts exist in my mind, my body, and in my experiences.

Love floods my consciousness with health, and every cell in my body is filled with light and healing energy.

After filling in with affirmations of your choice, use this final statement to end your affirmations as you drift into a deep sleep:

I am going into a deep sleep and when I awake I am refreshed, calm and confident, knowing my life has improved as I move forward with fun activities, clarity in my decisions, wonderful relationships, good health, and activities that result in my unlimited wealth.

These are affirmations to use during the day, or in the middle of your nighttime tape:

I am giving just by being in this world, and receiving comes easily for me.

As I receive I bring joy to those who give to me.

I am exhilarated that my wealth allows me to impact the world positively by giving to charities, beautifying my environment, giving to others, and graciously receiving.

I am expanding my career with ease.

As I let go to outcomes and serve others I experience personal growth and success.

I am focused and clear.

I make decisions easily.

I am clear about who I am and what makes me happy.

Large sums of money come to me quickly, under grace, in perfect ways.

I am delighted to be known as an expert in my field.

I am always pleased how easy it is for me to learn new information.

I am confident.

I move forward rapidly, always trusting in myself.

I am able to honor my feelings at all times.

I am my best friend and take care to nurture and support my feelings, my body, my lifestyle, my relationships, and my good fortune.

My checking account grows larger and larger each day.

I receive unexpected money.

I receive easily.

I am a money magnet.

I attract money to me easily.

I always have more money than I can spend.

I am an excellent speaker, well prepared, logical, confident, and completely at ease before any group.

I have knowledge of my subject and an intense desire to share my knowledge with others.

I am easily able to relax as deeply as I wish at all times.

I smile and laugh easily.

I am feeling and looking younger, more vibrant, and energetic each day.

I choose healthy foods and activities that allow me to be slim and energetic.

I am clear about my true destiny.

I am enjoying how everything flows easily for me.

I am enjoying a wonderful business, and I give wonderful service, for wonderful pay!

I am relaxed and confident.

I take action, always knowing what brings me success and joy.

I am supported and surrounded by talented and successful people.

I can handle whatever happens to me, in any given situation.

I am a good communicator.

I am a good listener.

I am in alignment with the Universe.

I am finding my work to be more and more fun, and am greatly rewarded each day.

I am grateful for the many lives I can benefit.

People love to give me money. I love to receive money.

I am a winner, I win often and I win big.

I am enjoying an abundance of great relationships.

I am clear about my life, goals, and career.

I am making new friends everywhere I go.

I am living a balanced life.

I am excited about all the travel I am able to do, and the beautiful places I get to see.

I have lots of fun with family.

I am calm and cheerful.

I am laughing a lot.

I know that God provides everything, the people, events, and support to achieve my desires.

I am moving forward rapidly.

I am able to take fun and enjoyable vacations whenever I want.

I am enjoying lots of friends and often receive invitations for fun activities.

I am elated to have _____ dollars in my checking (or savings) account and always have money to pay for the things I desire.

I am thankful for good health.

I am thankful for the good health of my family.

I am thankful for a flexible schedule where I enjoy fun activities. My desires fall in place easily and effortlessly.

I am thankful for the loving relationships in my life.

I am cherished by those I love.

I am thankful I receive support through people, ideas, creativity, good health, and wealth.

I am thankful I am surrounded with love and joy.

I am enjoying an exhilarating life!

I am relaxed, confident, comfortable and calm wherever I am.

No matter what is going on in the world, I am safe. My family is in a safe place at all times.

Chapter Exercises

Chapter One
Exercise 1:

Think of something you really enjoyed, a trip to Disneyland with your family, a trip to a wonderful destination overseas, your wedding or the wedding of a close friend, a first trip to Las Vegas when you were dazzled by all the lights. Maybe your joy came from a time you enjoyed nature while camping with your family or friends, or the time you won a door prize, or won something you really desired.

Now that you have the event in mind, think about what you did and how you felt. It is particularly important to observe and remember your feelings. Write what you were feeling on a piece of paper. Was it the feeling of love, passion, excitement, or exhilaration? All of these feelings carry motion with them. While daydreaming about the experience, you may notice the good feelings moving through your body, the very motion that creates more of those good things to come into your life.

It is important when you create to be able to connect with these positive emotions. If you can remember how those positive emotions felt, then you can recreate them when you want to attract something new into your life, whether it is a new relationship, an increase in income, or a terrific vacation.

Exercise 2:

Think about something that was embarrassing to you, or sad, or upsetting. Can you feel the emotion within your body? You may even feel pain in certain areas of your body. Your heart may start to race, or the muscles in your arms or legs may start to hurt. It is important for you to become aware of the movement of this emotional energy going to various parts of your body: this non-physical energy. You can feel it, but you cannot physically see it.

Whenever you notice your attention has moved to something unpleasant in your past, you can journal about it until you have exhausted the feelings, or you can choose to change your focus and turn to something that is pleasant, preferably something you are looking forward to, something you are excited about creating, or doing. Either way, you are doing what it takes to be able to "let go" of the experience, journaling until you are tired of recalling the event, or thinking about something pleasant. It could be a trip, a home remodeling project, or something as simple as attending a party or going to a movie. Be sure to recall a pleasant thought that evokes good feelings before moving on to the rest of this book.

Exercise 3:

Using the positive feelings and emotions you have just recalled, take a spiral notebook and pen to a quiet peaceful place and sit down and relax. Whether it's a favorite spot in your home, the beach, a place in nature, your garden, or the local park, make sure it's a place you will be able to totally relax without being interrupted. Begin by asking yourself, "If I were to do something that is really fun and enjoyable, what would it be?" Allow your mind to wander. If you have any thoughts that distract you, allow them to float away from your mind.

Now is your opportunity to write your own script, your opportunity to write it the way you would like to live it. For this first experience, choose something you believe could happen rather easily. As you start to get a picture of something that would be fun to do or have, allow yourself to experience that through your emotions. Feel the excitement, joy, and passion, allowing any feelings about your desire to come forward. Begin to journal the experience in detail. When you have completely exhausted yourself with every detail and really felt the emotions of the experience, put down your pen and close the notebook. Now let it go. Do not attempt to think about how this experience may come into your life. The key here is to let it go and allow it to be brought back to you.

Chapter Two
Exercise 1:

To help you get clear about your own preferences, take out a piece of paper and begin by making a list of events in your life that made you giggle. List things throughout your life, from a very young age until now, that brought you pleasure, joy, or laughter. As you make your list, notice if you were doing something with someone, or were you alone? Was it a passive activity like sitting by a lake and fishing, or was it an activity like swimming or skiing? Begin at the earliest age you can remember and think of joyful moments. Write them down.

Take as long as you need to get as many activities listed as possible. Once the list is complete, go back and see if you have similar activities reoccurring over and over all your life. If not, you may be the type who has to have lots of variety. Or maybe you have to be doing something creative: building or designing. What about people? When you were having the most fun, were you with family, friends, or co-workers? Or were you all by yourself?

Remember not to judge the experience, just allow yourself to get to know your preferences: likes and dislikes. This exercise will help you make quicker decisions for yourself in the future. Our experiences give us information about what we enjoy and what we dislike. To experience something and fail is far better than to have never experienced it at all.

Exercise 2:

This exercise helps to change unwanted habits. If you have someone you spend a lot of time with, it would be helpful to ask them to help you with this exercise. This will help you realize how your words may be holding you back from moving forward to create a magical life. Words are a reflection of your thoughts and habits. Ask someone to keep track of every time you use the word ***should or try***. If you are caught using either of these words, then you will need to give up something in order to become more aware and change this habit. You might choose to put $1 in a jar for a charitable donation, or give up something important to you each time you are caught slipping.

I heard on TV that a famous actress used this technique by having her father catch her in a behavior she wanted to change. She had two small children and wanted to stop cursing. To stop the habit, her father suggested she let go of something important to her, like the frequent purchase of new shoes. Because she loved new shoes, she quickly changed her bad habit.

It is important for you to select something you care enough about losing that motivates you to change your habit. Practice this exercise over a twenty-one-day period, because studies have shown it often takes a minimum of twenty-one days to change a habit. If you are consistent, you will begin to change your thoughts and your words.

Exercise 3:

This is a simple exercise to help you form the habit of focusing on creating what you want each day. In this chapter I refer to using a "God can" because it helps to remind you that "God can" handle your requests. You may choose to name it "Angel can" or "Spirit can", just find the best way for you to reinforce the action of letting go and turning your requests over to the invisible. You can name your can anything that resonates with support. Find a shoebox, glass jar, or a large can.

Your container needs to have a lid and be large enough to hold at least fifty folded pieces of paper. Cut a slit about two or three inches long in your lid. When you begin your morning, sit for ten minutes and jot down on a piece of paper whatever comes into your mind that you desire for that day, week, or month. If you have children, you can get them in the habit of doing this before going to bed. Let them decorate their container and make it a fun family project. Each person needs to have a separate container and it is best not to share the experience you asked for until it has occurred.

If you are new to this method of manifesting from your thoughts using directed intention, I suggest you start with simple requests, because you will get faster demonstrations and increase your belief in the process. Some suggestions: write that you would like to experience laughter throughout your day, that you would like to receive a surprise phone call from someone you have longed to speak with, or perhaps receive an invitation to a party or for a lunch date. Just as I had asked for music to come into my son's life in a positive way, your request must not indicate how the demonstration will appear. Let go of all attachment to the result.

Once you have written one request on a piece of paper, fold the paper and put it in the container and forget about it. Do not think of the request again. You may be surprised at the requests you wrote, and how many actually become part of your daily activities. Make as many requests each day as you would like during the ten minutes you spend. After a week or two, you can pull out your notes and review what you had written. Remember to visualize the activity and think about how you would feel if it occurred. Remember that joyful feelings and thoughts about your desires create faster results. Anything that has not been created can be placed back in the box or replaced with a clearer intention.

Chapter Three
Exercise 1:

Give yourself about a half hour for this exercise. Sit down in a quiet spot where you will not be interrupted. Once you are relaxed, think about someone in your life who has made a positive impact on you. This person can be dead or living. Even if you feel you have shared your feelings with this person, write down all the things that come to mind about them that have made you grateful for their influence on your life.

If more than one person comes to mind, you may want to write about a different person each day in order to give this exercise the importance it deserves. Once you have written your list, contact the person and share how you feel with them. You may be surprised at the positive impact this exercise has on their life. If the person is deceased, read your list out loud to yourself or someone close to you. You may be surprised at the positive impact this has on your own life.

Chapter Four
Exercise 1:

Are you a giver or receiver? Do you always have to be the one to give? Often, giving gives us a feeling of control over others, or gives us a feeling of power over our own circumstances. Perhaps you feel sorry for others and feel you need to take care of them. This exercise will help you create balance in giving and receiving. The best way you can gain more abundance in your life is to be able to receive as much as you are able to give. If you tend to be the one always receiving and being taken care of, then it may be your turn to give. Let go of the idea that others need to take care of you. By giving more, it shows the Universe you trust there will always be enough in your life.

Decide if you are fearful of giving or receiving. Decide if you tend to be out of balance in one or the other. Then spend the week giving spontaneously if you have determined you are a receiver, or spend the week receiving if you tend to be a giver.

Give in accordance with your income and your level of trust. Do not do anything that will place you in financial hardship or anxiety. Just be aware of what you are giving and receiving, and how you feel about it. This exercise is to increase your awareness of how you experience life.

Do you only give when you feel you have more than enough? Do you give compliments easily? When you have a desire to give, do you act spontaneously or analyze first before giving? Observe any self-talk going on in your head.

Ways that you might give: Ask to pay for the car in line behind you as you drive through a fast food location, or offer to pay for the coffee or the ice cream order when in a snack shop. How about a smile or a positive acknowledgement to someone who may need a lift? At first you may find changing a habit feels very uncomfortable. How about offering your letter carrier a soda or bottle of water? If you have a favorite charity you always give to, why not increase your donation, or choose an additional charity.

Be prepared to receive. When offered a compliment, immediately say thank you and don't debate the compliment. When a friend wants to buy you lunch or treat you be gracious and accept. Watch to see the benefits that come to you as you seek balance in the area of giving and receiving.

Chapter Five
Exercise 1:

It is important to know and be honest with yourself in order to create a magical life. Prioritize the following values, with your first choice on top: doing the right thing, money, control, helping people, family, friends, education, learning new information. Do not judge the order you choose, and do not pick what you think would be socially acceptable.

Write down what you feel you would like to create for your life after you get clear in your mind what it is you truly want. What would bring you the most joy? Consider what you are doing, or have done to achieve your desire. Ask yourself what are you doing that is in conflict with your desire. Ask yourself how you sabotage your goals.

List the things you do that could be keeping your goal from occurring. For example, you may resist clearing your clutter at home or in the office. The clutter problem could be keeping you from experiencing something you fear, like: making an important decision, working on a project that feels overwhelming or beyond your ability, or the fear of throwing something of value away that you believe you might need later need, lacking a trust within yourself to easily obtain the information when needed. All of these fears are based on underlying beliefs. Once you have identified the belief, you can decide what action you can take to change. Start with small steps to gain comfort in your new actions.

If you need help changing the habit, don't hesitate to ask the Universe to send you someone to help. Then watch for someone to appear. Allowing someone to help you is a sign that you are able to receive, and it gives you practice to allow the support. When you allow the support from others, the Universe continues to send you more blessing and support.

Leave yourself encouraging affirmations on your bathroom mirror, by your nightstand, or in your car to remind you of your newly desired action. Be good to yourself, knowing and allowing for a relapse. If you find yourself going back to the old habit, be sure to replace it with your newly desired behavior as soon as possible.

If an action you need to take is something you do not want to do, consider a person who would help. Be willing to pay for help from others, and trust that your time is valuable. Remember, if the task is something you do not enjoy, you may be avoiding it on an unconscious level, and that avoidance can cost the achievement of your goal. You now know what it is you will need to receive, so go to your "God can," as explained in Chapter Two, and add what you need. The Universe is waiting for you to ask. These requests could include having a wonderful job in a great environment doing only what you enjoy, having a very supportive assistant to accomplish what you don't prefer

218

to do, or having a loving and supportive relationship with someone you trust and with whom you feel truly connected.

Exercise 2:

Creation follows thought. In this exercise you will be able to get clear and allow yourself to see that what you are asking for is already present in your life. Take a piece of paper and write what you want at the top:

(Use one sheet only for each desire)

Below, on the same side of the paper list the reasons why you want it:

Leave the whole bottom of the paper to write all the feelings you think you would have if you had it. Be sure to focus on the feelings.

On the backside of the paper, write the reasons you believe you already have it:

It is said that even before you ask, your desire will be answered. Creation follows thought, which follows perception. If you can perceive that you already have what you are asking for, it will be easy to keep that desire coming. It increases your belief of possibility. Intuitive counselors see how you are living and believing today and are able to reasonably predict a similar situation occurring for you. An honest intuitive will tell you that you can change anything you are experiencing by changing your thoughts about it.

For this exercise, if you want to have a better relationship with someone, write down your desire. Example: I want to have a better relationship with my neighbor. Write why you want it. Example: It feels good to have someone you know and can count on living close-by. It is feels good to know people care. It would bring a feeling of safety knowing my neighbor. List all the feelings you would have if you had a better relationship with your neighbor. Turn over the paper and list all the reasons you believe you already have what you desire. Example: My neighbor waves when I drive by. My neighbor is respectful of my sleeping hours. I have asked to borrow some eggs from my neighbor and they were glad to loan them. My neighbor helped me find my lost pet. This exercise will help you increase your belief about having what you want.

Start this exercise with desires that can be validated, which also helps increase your gratitude and brings in more of what you desire.

Exercise 3:

This exercise is important to do without analyzing. Just complete each sentence below with one word.

1.   People who are rich are

_____.

2.   Teenagers who drive new cars are

_____.

3.   People who have a college degree are
_____.

4.   People who shop a lot are
_____.

5.   People who leave their children with babysitters are
_____.

6.   People who take vacations every year are
_____.

7.   Women who are thin are
_____.

8.   Men who watch sports all weekend are
_____.

9.   People who go to the gym and exercise regularly are
_____.

10.   People who go snow skiing are
_____.

11.   People who play tennis a lot are
_____.

12.   People who go camping with their family are
_____.

13.   People who wear expensive jewelry are
_____.

14.   People who sleep in late are
_____.

15.   People who get up early are
_____.

16.   People who work in an 8-5 job five days a week are
_____.

17. People who work all their life in the same job will
_____.

18. People who own their own business are
_____.

19. People who own their own home are
_____.

20. People who live in apartments are
_____

21. People who wear glasses are
_____.

22. People who talk with an accent are
_____.

23. Men who have beards are
_____.

24. People that are tall are
_____.

25. People who are short are
_____.

You can make up your own sentences. You will find your judgment keeps you from having what you want. If you believe that people who have wealth are more likely to be workaholics, you may not want to have wealth. If you feel that teenagers who drive new cars are spoiled, you may not want to be seen in a new car.

This exercise is to show you how your mind judges and will resist having the very thing you say you want in order to avoid an underlying fear or to maintain a certain belief.

Chapter 6
Exercise 1:

Carry a note pad with you throughout the day and write down every time you agree to do something you really do not want to do. You will need to become your own best friend. You will need to acknowledge your own personal feelings and trust how you are feeling for this exercise to be successful for you.

At the end of the day before going to bed, find some quiet time and review your notes. Take time to ask yourself, "What would happen if I had said no?" Are you coming from fear of loss that you may lose another person's love? Are you coming from a place of feeling obligated? Are you doing something you don't want to do because you have been told you should? Do you think you need to please others? Do you feel responsible for another's happiness?

Ask yourself these questions and get clear what it is that drives your decisions. If it is to please someone else, then you are not living your life to the fullest degree possible and you are denying yourself the opportunity to enjoy being who you really are. You are cheating yourself of life. The responsibility for your own happiness is completely up to you.

Chapter Seven
Exercise 1:

This is a fun exercise to build your intuition, and these cards are sold in most bookstores. You will need to purchase a deck of angel cards, Zen cards, animal cards, or any deck of cards that have intuitive messages and colorful pictures. Use your cards before you meditate, or before you need to make an important decision, or just for fun. After selecting your deck of cards, find a place where you can be alone to access your own intuition and focus on the cards. Shuffle the cards while asking a question. Your question could be: *What do I need to focus on right now in my life? What do I need to be more aware of at this time?* Or just allow the information you might need to receive to come in without asking a question. Keep shuffling the cards until one just falls into your lap. It is best to read only one card at a time. If more than three cards fall out, put them back and reshuffle. If you were supposed to receive the message on those cards, it will come in again.

Chapter Eight
Exercise 1:

Without going to a hypnotherapist, sit down with a notebook and pen. Take a deep breath and relax, then take two more deep breaths and relax. Clear your mind by letting go of your thoughts. If anything comes into your mind that is distracting you from relaxing, attach that thought to the visualization of a helium balloon and allow it to float away. Concentrate on breathing in and out, and relax.

Once you're relaxed, read and answer the questions below without analyzing them. Realize and trust that your intention to receive information about an existing challenge in your life will produce clarity and the answers you need to move forward. Without judging it, write down the first answer that comes into your mind as soon as you receive the information.

Do the exercise as if you are a child playing a fun game of imagination. If it is difficult for you to believe in a past life, then picture yourself recalling a dream or a vision, or as if you are acting in a movie or play you may have seen sometime. When you are relaxed and ready, begin to read and write the answers to these questions.

1. Where is your vision taking place: what country or location?
2. Were you a male or female?
3. How old were you?
4. What were you wearing?
5. When you are satisfied with that image, move to an important event in that life. Write about that event, giving as much detail as you can.
6. How do you make a living in that life? Or is there something specific you do everyday?
7. Who were the other people in your life?
8. Imagine yourself in various events of that life where you felt sad or upset and describe that occasion or event. Take as long as you need write everything down.
9. Write about a joyful time in that life.

10. If there is anything else you need to know about that experience, write it down.
11. Advance to the time when you died and describe that moment. Was it quick? Were you in a place of your choosing? Who was with you at the time?
12. Picture yourself passing and in a peaceful place. What did you learn from that life and those experiences? What would you like to change about that life if you could? What was the one thing you learned from that life?
13. See if anything you wrote is similar to the life you are living now. Are your beliefs related to anything in this past life vision?
14. Did you gain any new understanding about the choices you are making today?

Chapter Nine
Exercise 1:

I suggest you consider a session with a hypnotherapist; it need not be one to explore past lives. You may find it very relaxing and helpful for any area of your life causing you some challenges. Another suggestion is to purchase a recording to do your own independent guided hypnosis. I have found Dick Sutphen's "Past Life Regression" CD to be very beneficial, but you may choose to do your own exploring on the Internet.

Chapter Ten
Exercise 1:

Look back over your life and list the movies you have enjoyed the most. Did you pick movies that brought you laughter, or ones with strong moral messages? Did you choose a drama, a romantic story, or one with an historical theme? Then see how this movie represents a mirror of your life or your desires or your personality. The movie can give you great insight about yourself and your personal preferences and help you make important future decisions regarding career options, hidden desires, and relationship issues that may have been hidden within your subconscious mind.

Chapter Eleven
Exercise 1:

For this exercise you will need a tape recorder in order to tape affirmations so that you can listen to them when going to sleep at night or during the daytime while driving, exercising, or doing housework. For positive affirmations refer to the back of this book for suggestions. I have found it is very important how your affirmations are worded. It is also important to add an emotional verb before your affirmation such as: *I am excited to receive a steady flow of income that allows me to live my dreams.* Be sure to put your affirmations in the present tense. By beginning your affirmation with "I am," you reinforce your desire and confidence.

The affirmations are done to raise your vibration and place a positive thought in your subconscious mind. When you add an emotional verb to your affirmation, it helps create excitement and energy around your desires. Once you have your list of affirmations written out, then tape record them in your own voice with soft music in the background.

Music also has vibration: positive and not so positive. It has been said that classical music has a very high positive vibration. That could be why surgeons often listen to classical music while doing surgery. Be sure the music you select helps you relax because you will be listening to it as you fall asleep. You will find this recording will also allow you to go to sleep easily and have a much deeper sleep. By listening to positive affirmations in your own voice, you replace any anxiety in your mind that may hinder your progress.

If you find affirmations boring and too repetitious for you, be more creative by describing the way your life will be when you have accomplished your present goals and desires. Walk through your entire day as if your dreams have already occurred, giving as much detail and emotion to describing the life you want to live. It's almost like writing a novel or a script with you being the main character. Be sure to listen to the tape every night as you fall asleep. The recording is best if it is 20 to 30 minutes in length. If you fall asleep while listening that is fine, because the affirmations and positive desires will go into your subconscious even if you are asleep. See the affirmations section at the back of this book for instructions for daytime or nighttime recording.

Chapter Twelve
Exercise 1:

The Universe, what some refer to as angels, your magical inner self, or what others call God is that magical energy that helps to manifest your world. If we acknowledge and recognize the magic that comes to us each day, we will begin to attract more to us. Some have suggested keeping a gratitude journal and that would work well for this exercise. The more grateful you become and the more you acknowledge your gratitude, the more things come to you to be grateful for.

Start a journal of magical occurrences. A magical occurrence is a synchronicity that happens when you feel you are in the right place at the right time and everything just seems to go smoothly for you.

This exercise will help you to not only identify the magic around you that is occurring all the time; it will increase your awareness, your intuition and help you to understand how to tap into the magic all the time. This exercise helps you form habits that will help your life flow effortlessly. This exercise will help you to trust and let go of the old habits of having to work hard to make something happen.

Think a positive thought and let go. You may want to record the successes that have occurred from your God Can requests from Chapter Four. Give your request time and watch what occurs. Then be sure to add the experience to your journal. Your writings will help increase your belief of possibilities, allowing you to expand your creations, and will help you reinforce that you are being supported by an infinite power, far greater than anything we could imagine or describe in words.

If you keep this notebook near your bed, you can record these occurrences at the end of your day. You can also use the book to keep track of any dreams you may have had, and to list those things you are grateful for. By writing your dreams immediately upon awakening, whether it's during the middle of the night or in the morning, it is important to jot down as much as you can remember about the specific dream. Our dreams bring us wisdom and insight, increasing our awareness, and help us to release stress and challenges we deal with in our everyday lives and human experiences.

Chapter Thirteen
Exercise 1:

Making a vision board, always a pleasure to do as a group exercise, will be a fun creative project. Studies have shown that pictures viewed regularly go deep into the subconscious mind and help attract what you desire into your life. Cut pictures and positive words out of a magazine and paste them on a poster board. Put all the things you desire on the board to make a beautiful collage. You can add actual pictures of family and friends. If you want to get slimmer, cut out a picture of a slim body and glue a picture of your face on it.

Be sure to include pictures that illustrate perfect health and vitality, fun activities and hobbies, places you might like to travel, the amount of income you would enjoy having in your bank account, words indicating financial freedom, or being a multi-millionaire. Include the type of home you would love to live in and the car you would enjoy driving. You may even want to visit your local dealership and be photographed sitting in your dream car.

Remember to list charities that you would like to support and any other things you desire to attract into your life. When you finish your vision board, have it reduced and photo copied in color to carry in your date book, post at your office, or have with you at all times in your briefcase. I have my vision board in my office above my computer so I can view it easily all the time. It is good to make a new vision board regularly. If you have children, encourage them to make their own vision boards.

Chapter Fourteen
Exercise 1:

Make a list of all the ways you treat yourself. Think of things you choose to do that give you support. Do you find your list is lean? If so, begin to make a list of all the ways you can treat yourself. It could be that your list includes taking thirty minutes every day to exercise. Perhaps taking a swim in a pool, or taking a walk in nature, getting a soothing massage, or just relaxing in a spa. For some it might be to set aside time for a relaxing bath, or to purchase something you never purchase for yourself, like a special piece of jewelry, an inspiring book or perfume. Do anything that makes you feel supported. It could be to let go of cleaning your home once a week and hiring a cleaning crew to help you. It is important to continue to give yourself love doing something every day consistently that brings you joy and causes you to feel good abut yourself.

I welcome your letters. Write me with your comments as well as to share your personal spiritual stories of letting go to:

Pat Sendejas – Feng Shui 4 Balance
Post Office Box 4514
Westlake Village, CA. 91359-1514
E-mail: Pat@PatSendejas.com

For information on classes, scheduling a lecture, obtaining my books, or scheduling a consultation visit my Web Site at:
Web Site at: www.fengshui4balance.com

About The Author

Personal environments have always been a passion for Pat Sendejas, starting her own interior design business in 1977. She had no inkling her ideas would grow and transform from planning commercial and residential spaces to helping clients transform their lives.

Interior design led to a consulting business using Feng Shui, which works with natural energy, and then, instinctively, to spiritual transformation. *Letting Go to Create a Magical Life* is a new beginning for this designer, speaker, teacher and author, and offers unique insights into the popular ideas of the Law of Attraction.

Along with teaching Feng Shui workshops, Pat leads seminars to teach others how to transform their lives by letting go of old beliefs and going within to understand and appreciate themselves. She also hosts a weekly talk radio show: "Let Go and Grow" on contacttalkradio.com.

Pat has always been a positive thinker and has realized how our thoughts create our physical world. Her love for writing and creating won her the 2007 Apex Award of Excellence in design and communication for her website fengshui4balance.com.

"I consider myself a visionary," Pat says. "Working with energy to create a fulfilling life for myself has been a wonderful experience that I wish to keep sharing with others."

Born in Omaha, Nebraska, Pat has spent most of her life in Southern California. She's married to a retired Los Angeles City firefighter and is the mother of two grown sons.